Strategies in Emerging Markets

Strategies in Emerging Markets
A Case Book on Danish Multinational Corporations in China and India

By Michael W. Hansen, Marcus M. Larsen, Torben Pedersen, Bent Petersen and Peter Wad

Copenhagen Business School Press

Strategies in Emerging Markets
A Case Book on Danish Multinational Corporations in China and India

© Copenhagen Business School Press, 2010
Printed in Denmark by Scandinavian Books
Typeset: SL grafik
Cover design by Klahr | Graphic Design
1st edition 2010

ISBN 978-87-630-0236-3

Distribution:

Scandinavia
DBK, Mimersvej 4
DK-4600 Køge, Denmark
Tel +45 3269 7788
Fax +45 3269 7789

North America
International Specialized Book Services
920 NE 58th Street, Suite 300
Portland, OR 97213-3786
Tel +1 800 944 6190
Fax +1 503 280 8832
Email: orders@isbs.com

Rest of the World
Marston Book Services, P.O. Box 269
Abingdon, Oxfordshire, OX14 4YN, UK
Tel +44 (0) 1235 465500
Fax +44 (0) 1235 465655
Email: client.orders@marston.co.uk

All rights reserved. No part of this publication may be reproduced or used in any form or by any means - graphic, electronic or mechanical including photocopying, recording, taping or information storage or retrieval systems - without permission in writing from Copenhagen Business School Press at www.cbspress.dk

Preface

Many Danish companies have established themselves in China and India. In the coming years, more are likely to follow. While the media is continually reporting on this increasingly important aspect of Danish industry, little consolidated evidence of Danish companies' experiences in India and China exists in print. After researching and teaching on issues related to Danish companies in China and India for several years, we found it relevant to collect and consolidate some of these experiences in this book.

Although this text is designed to serve as a case book for students of international business and strategy, practitioners and managers working with and in emerging markets may find inspiration in these pages. The book has been written in English, as we believe that the experiences of the Danish companies in India and China are generalizable beyond the Danish context.

Although the book draws on our general knowledge about the case companies, it is based exclusively on public sources, such as articles in the business press and information provided by the companies on their home pages. The story lines and perspectives presented in the individual cases are based solely on our interpretation of the companies' strategies and activities, and they have not been approved or validated by the companies described. In order to encourage readers to adopt a decision maker's perspective, each case has a protagonist. However, any thoughts and motives ascribed to these protagonists are purely speculative.

We would like to thank Eskil Riskær, Githa Kurdahl and Ditte Salling for their dedicated research assistance in connection with the preparation of this book. We would also like to thank the Centre for Business and Development Studies at Copenhagen Business School and Fabrikejer, ingeniør Valdemar Selmer Trane og hustru, Elisa Tranes fond for financial support to the project.

Copenhagen, July 2010

TABLE OF CONTENTS

PREFACE · 5

CHAPTER 1
Introduction · 11
The rise of India and China · 11

A brief history of Danish industry in India and China · 12

Opportunities and challenges facing Danish investors in China and India · 13

An introduction to the cases · 14

What is special about MNC strategy in emerging markets? · 16

How the cases illustrate challenges and opportunities in emerging markets · 22

Conclusion · 25

CHAPTER 2
Carlsberg A/S
– Probably the best beer company in western China · 27
Introducing Carlsberg A/S · 28

Towards an emerging market strategy · 30

Carlsberg in China · 32

Exhibits for Carlsberg A/S case · 37

CHAPTER 3
ECCO A/S
– Producing the Dragon's footwear · 45
Introducing ECCO A/S · 46

ECCO's global value chain – "From Cow to Customer" · 47

ECCO A/S in China · 50

Dealing with the Dragon · 52

Exhibits for ECCO A/S case· 55

CHAPTER 4
Casting the global turnaround of FLSmidth – The Indian case · 69

The crises of FLSmidth · 69

FLSmidth: "One source – one partner" · 70

Casting the Indian case · 73

Implementing the Indian strategy · 75

Exhibits for FLSmidth A/S case· 81

CHAPTER 5
Bestseller – Facing a new competitive landscape in China · 93

Introducing Bestseller A/S · 94

Bestseller China · 97

The competitive challenges facing Bestseller China · 100

Exhibits for Bestseller A/S case· 105

CHAPTER 6
A.P. Møller Mærsk – Leveraging first-mover advantages in Vietnam · 119

A.P. Møller – Mærsk: a Danish conglomerate · 120

Mærsk's container business in Vietnam: Riding the economic wave · 125

Creating global opportunities for customers in Vietnam · 127

Exhibits for A.P. Møller Mærsk case· 131

CHAPTER 7
Vestas Wind Systems A/S – Changing winds in the Indian market for wind turbines · 139

Introducing Vestas Wind Systems A/S · 140

Vestas Wind Systems India Pvt. Ltd. · 142

The rise of Indian competitors · 146

Exhibits for Vestas Wind Systems A/S case· 149

CHAPTER 8
Danfoss in China
– Taking on the kingdom in the middle · 155

Introducing the Danfoss Group · 156

International orientation · 157

Danfoss in China: discovering the mid-end market · 158

Exhibits for Danfoss case· 165

LIST OF REFERENCES · 175

ENDNOTES · 181

CHAPTER 1

Introduction

This book presents seven studies of foreign direct investments (FDI) made by Danish multinational corporations' (MNCs) in China and India. The book focuses on the strategic challenges and opportunities that these MNCs face, and how they have dealt with those challenges and opportunities. By presenting the real-life experiences of Danish MNCs, and their strategies in China and India, we hope to inspire students and managers to critically consider this fascinating aspect of international business strategy. We also aim to spur debate about the engagement of Danish industry in emerging markets. This chapter briefly places the seven case studies in an empirical and theoretical context.

The rise of India and China

The world's economic map is currently being redrawn with the center of gravity shifting toward Asia. This process is largely driven by growing economic vitality and demographic developments in the two Asian giants, China and India. Together, these countries are home to 40 percent of the world's population. They are the world's second and fourth largest economies, respectively, in purchasing power parity (PPP) terms. They accounted for half of the growth in world GDP in the mid 2000s and they inject millions of consumers and workers into the global economy every year. Although India and China have also been hit by the recent global financial crisis, the two countries appear to remain on their growth trajectories of 5% to 10% annual GDP growth. They are likely to emerge from the financial crisis in a stronger position vis-à-vis other countries.

The rise of the Asian giants fundamentally changes the strategic landscape for MNCs. Most MNCs – regardless of whether they are large or small, in manufacturing or services, old or new, suppliers or brand holders – must, in one way or another, take India and China's rapidly growing markets, seemingly limitless human resources and increasingly competent local industries into consideration. MNCs must decide whether they wish to take a risk and enter these markets at an early stage, or wait until the markets and infrastructures have matured. They must consider whether and how they should modify sales, marketing and delivery systems to fit the particular market conditions and consumer preferences of the Asian giants. They must decide whether they should confront rising Chinese and Indian competitors in their home markets before they grow too strong. They must contemplate whether to offshore parts of their value chains to India and China, and they must consider whether complex activities, such as research, development and design, should be conducted in these countries. This book allows readers to closely examine how seven Danish MNCs have tackled these and other strategic challenges and opportunities in China and India.

A brief history of Danish industry in India and China

The presence of Danish industry and commerce in Asia is not a recent phenomenon. The Asian Company (originally chartered by Danish King Christian IV in 1616 as the "Danish East India Company") administered trade with the Danish colonies and trading posts in India (Trankebar, Frederiksnagore and Serampore) in the seventeenth and eighteenth centuries. The first Danish merchant ship arrived at the Pearl River in China in 1676. By 1772, the Danish East India Company had a monopoly on Danish trade with China and it established a trading post in Canton (now Guangzhou). In 1884, H. N. Andersen set up a private trading company in Bangkok that later became the East Asian Company (EAC). Throughout the late nineteenth and early twentieth centuries, the EAC established a string of trade representatives in Asia, built shipping routes to China and India, and integrated backward and forward into new activities, such as plantations, and the production and sale of consumer goods. Moreover, large Danish engineering companies, such as Monberg & Thorsen, Højgaard & Schulz and Great Northern Telegraph, were present in India and China in the late 19th and early 20th century, where they built bridges, roads, telegraph lines and power stations. FLSmidth, a producer of equipment for cement plants, entered China (Hong Kong) and India (Madras) in the early twentieth century. In fact, the largest Indian engineering company today, Larsen & Toubro, was established in 1938 by two FLSmidth engineers stationed in India.

In the wake of the Chinese Communist Revolution of 1949, the assets of several Danish companies, including the EAC, were confiscated by the government. Increasingly inward-looking policies in India also made life difficult for Danish MNCs, which, as a result, largely abandoned the country. However, as China and India started to open their economies in the 1980s after decades of inward-looking industrial policies, a group of Danish firms responded with investments. Among the early movers in India were Danfoss (in the 1960s), FLSmidth (1984), MarinPlast (1984), Asian Can (1989) and Asian Closures (1989). Their counterparts in China were EAC (1987), Codan Gummi (1987), Krüger (1988) and GN Resound (1989).

However, it was not until the mid 1990s that Danish investment in the two countries took off in earnest, spurred by a number of factors: liberalization of requirements for foreign investors (both countries), establishment of special economic zones (mainly China), drastic reductions in tariffs (both countries), enormous investments in infrastructure (mainly China), and rapidly growing purchasing power (both countries). By 2008, more than 300 Danish companies had established operations through FDI in China, while the corresponding figure for India was almost 100. In addition, a large number of firms dealt with these countries through other arrangements, such as outsourcing, strategic alliances, licensing and franchising. Among the largest Danish investors in China were Novozymes, Carlsberg Breweries, Sonion, A.P. Møller – Mærsk, Danisco Ingredients, Arla Foods, ECCO, Grundfoss, Danfoss and Vestas. In India, FLSmidth & Co., Carlsberg Breweries, Cowi, Vestas, Group 4, A.P. Møller – Mærsk, Roulund's Rubber, Grundfos, Danfoss and Danisco were large investors.

Opportunities and challenges facing Danish investors in China and India

The small size of the Danish domestic market and its limited human resource base make it particularly important for Danish companies to access the vast potential offered by the Asian giants. Moreover, as many Danish firms – especially those that act as suppliers and subcontractors to large MNCs in business-to-business (BtB) markets – are under growing pressure from customers to reduce costs, they increasingly need to explore the possibility of lowering costs through offshoring to low-cost locations like India and China.

Launching operations in India and China is not a problem-free endeavor, however. Many investments have gone awry: joint ventures that started as happy marriages ended in bitter divorces; overly optimistic assessments of future market opportunities led to subsidiaries struggling to just break even; failures to understand local legal systems resulted in MNCs finding their trademarks and patents violated; and large investments were, in some instances, lost due to unanticipated government decisions. Perhaps as a consequence of the above, many Danish companies have been reluctant to commit to the Asian giants. Industry associations and export promotion agencies alike report that Danish industry could do much better in India and China. Danish trade and investment relations with India and China are still relatively underdeveloped compared to other small open economies, and most Danish MNCs still appear to regard these countries as reservoirs of cheap, unsophisticated inputs, rather than future key markets or potential bases for advanced activities, such as R&D. This book, therefore, provides insights into how seven Danish MNCs have seized the opportunities and addressed the challenges of doing business in India and China. By sharing the experiences of these flagship firms, this collection of cases may inform and inspire firms and managers that are contemplating entry into these countries.

Strategies in emerging markets

An introduction to the cases

We have chosen to present seven cases, each of which covers a Danish MNC with significant activity in India and China. These are Carlsberg (China), FLSmidth (India), ECCO (China and Asia), Bestseller (China), Vestas (India) and Danfoss (China). The seventh case focuses on APM-Maersk's entry into Vietnam, but it relates explicitly to the challenges posed by China's rising shipping industry. The cases represent a broad range of Danish MNCs in terms of industries, market segments and value-chain activities. They are, however, not fully representative of Danish industry per se. In the Danish context, they are all relatively large MNCs with significant prior internationalization experience and they all have long-standing activities in China and India.

Carlsberg

In the early part of this century, the 140-year-old Danish brewery Carlsberg was facing mounting challenges due to intensifying competition in the beer industry and strong consolidation pressure. The company risked becoming the target of a hostile takeover or, alternatively, being cornered as a small regional player. However, turnaround efforts were successful and, by 2008, Carlsberg was among the five largest breweries in the world. Central to the turnaround was an ambitious acquisition strategy applied in emerging markets, such as Russia, Eastern Europe and China. The case presented in this book focuses on Carlsberg's entry into China, which started as a commercial failure in the eastern part of the country but subsequently developed successfully in the west.

FLSmidth

The large Danish producer of equipment for mineral processing, FLSmidth, faced a number of challenges in the early 2000s. Its market shares were falling, its losses were mounting, its owners were entrenched in internal warfare and the company had diversified into a large number of unprofitable business segments. By 2004, a new management team devised a new strategy. Among the key pillars in this strategy was the rapid expansion of the company's Indian subsidiary with a view to making India a global sourcing platform for engineering services. Within a few years, the Indian operation grew to become the largest engineering site of FLSmidth and had almost 3,000 employees. This case demonstrates, *inter alia,* how management's commitment was absolutely crucial to the successful expansion of the company's Indian activities.

ECCO

ECCO, the large Danish shoe producer, was one of the first Danish companies to commit to a global sourcing strategy, which started with Portugal in the 1970s, and moved to encompass Indonesia and Thailand in the 1980s. The company has

Introduction

built five factories in China since 2000. ECCO has, contrary to its competitors, pursued an internalization strategy in which sourcing has been overwhelmingly organized in-house. The case deals with ECCO's massive investment in China, the reasons for its strong Chinese commitment and how it successfully interacted with the authorities in China.

Bestseller
In 1996, two Danish entrepreneurs based in China convinced Troels Holck Povlsen, the founder and former president of the garment retail company Bestseller, to establish a (small) joint venture in China aimed at introducing the Bestseller brands to the region. By 2008, the Chinese activities had evolved into a giant operation with more than 2,000 outlets and 15,000 employees, and Bestseller was one of the absolute market leaders. The Bestseller case highlights how the company engaged in a successful market entry and became a market leader, and how it geared up to defend its incumbent position in the Chinese market against low-cost Asian producers.

A.P. Møller – Mærsk
As the world's largest container shipping company, A.P. Møller – Mærsk needs to be able to offer services to its clients around the globe, including those in emerging markets. Often, however, emerging markets lack the infrastructure and business regulation needed to support shipping and logistics activities. The case demonstrates how A.P. Møller – Mærsk built a logistics and shipping network from scratch in Vietnam, and how it worked with local authorities to gain a lead over its competitors. Furthermore, the case illustrates how A.P. Møller – Mærsk creates value for global MNCs by offering door-to-door logistics and transport services and, in the process, integrates Vietnamese industries into global value chains. The case ends with an account of the challenges A.P. Møller – Mærsk faces in Asia stemming from low-cost Chinese competitors.

Vestas
India is the world's fifth-largest producer of wind energy and, correspondingly, the Indian markets is of remarkable size. While Vestas, the world's largest wind turbine manufacture, was present in India at an early stage, it never succeeded in becoming a market leader. On the contrary, Vestas watched as its position was surpassed by several Indian windmill manufacturers. Among these were the local wind turbine producer Suzlon, which became a major competitor on a global scale. The case traces this initial Indian failure back to "path dependence" caused by the mode of entry – a joint venture with an Indian partner. The partnership was riddled with problems, and when Vestas and NEG Micon merged in 2003, Vestas withdrew from its Indian joint venture and put its stake into

NEG Micon's fully controlled Indian subsidiary. Recently, Vestas has upgraded its commitment to India, as it views India as not only a large market but also as a potential sourcing platform. For example, Vestas has established an R&D subsidiary in India that sources engineering and technical services for its global R&D centre.

Danfoss

Danfoss, a producer of control systems for cooling and heating, was present in China at an early stage of the country's economic liberalization process. After some initial problems, the company successfully entered the Chinese premium market. The case, however, deals with the mid-market segment in China, which was mainly occupied by local producers. Danfoss became increasingly concerned that potential competitors would emerge from the mid-market segment and encroach upon Danfoss' dominant position in the premium market. Consequently, the company, in contrast to its activities in other emerging markets, pursued a strategy adapted to the Chinese mid-market. The benefits, as well as dangers, of this strategy form the core of this case.

What is special about MNC strategy in emerging markets?

Firm strategy is about "capturing what the manager learns from all sources (both the soft insights from his or her personal experiences and the experiences of others throughout the organization and the hard data from market research and the like) and then synthesizing that learning into a vision of the direction that the business should pursue" (Mintzberg, 1994; 107). Some strategy schools focus more on the firm's external environment, including industry, market or institutional environments, in the formulation of strategy (the outside-in perspective), while others focus more on the characteristics of the firm, such as resources and capabilities, in the formulation of strategy (the inside-out perspective) (Hoskisson et al., 1998). Global strategy[1] is essentially about strategies of firms that operate in more than one country, most of which are MNCs (Tallman, 2006).

MNCs face a number of strategic choices that are distinct to their multinationality: which locations they should internationalize to (Dunning, 1988; Mudambi, 1995); which functions should be internationalized (Porter, 1986; Buckley and Ghauri, 2004); whether foreign activities should be organized in-house or externally (Buckley and Casson, 1976; Hennart, 1991); which entry mode should be adopted (Anderson and Gatignon, 1986; Madhok, 1997); which products should be sold where and how (Levitt, 1987; Douglas and Craig, 1989); how knowledge processes should be organized across borders (Kogut and Zander, 1993; Grant et al, 2000); how relations between domestic and foreign operations should be organized (Bartlett and Ghoshal, 1988; Birkinshaw, 1998); how cultural issues should be managed across locations and functions (Hofstede, 1983; Trompenaars and Hampden-Turner, 1998); how foreign activities should be fi-

Introduction

nancially appraised and financed (Buckley, 1986; Shapiro, 2003); at what speed and with what commitment internationalization should take place (Johanson and Vahlne, 1977; McDougall et al., 1994); and in general, what role different locations should be assigned in the overall strategy of the firm (Kogut, 1985; Hamel and Prahalad, 1985). These and other choices are what constitute global strategy (Laserre, 2007).

The strategies of MNCs are, to some degree, shaped and dictated by the characteristics of the particular location in which they are operating. This book deals specifically with two emerging market locations: India and China. While the distinct histories, political systems and business systems of India and China undoubtedly have significant implications for MNC strategizing related to the two countries (Tollentino, 2008), we argue that these two countries share some characteristics, as they are both *emerging markets*.[2] These characteristics may have important implications for MNC strategy. While we are aware that it is probably impossible to identify a single set of emerging market characteristics that affects MNC strategy, we argue that the distinctiveness of formulating and implementing strategy in emerging markets is related to at least four dimensions: the nature of markets, the nature of resource bases, the nature of institutions and the nature of competition.

The nature of markets

Several distinct aspects of the nature of emerging markets may affect the marketing strategy and marketing mix (Kotler, 1984) adopted by MNCs.

First, emerging markets typically show high growth rates (Arnold and Quelch, 1998) and, consequently, they are lucrative markets (especially the large ones) for MNCs compared to the relatively stagnant markets in developed countries. The continued high growth in several of these markets despite the financial crisis has increased their relative importance for MNCs (Kekic, 2009). In the long run, there is little doubt that many MNCs' market portfolios will tilt toward emerging markets (Cavusgil et al., 2002; Wright et al., 2005).

Second, the market structure in emerging markets is often different from the market structures in developed countries. For instance, we simultaneously find the existence of global, glocal, local and bottom of the pyramid (BOP) market segments in emerging markets (Khanna and Palepu, 2006). Currently, most MNCs prefer to operate in the global market segment (both in BtB and in consumer markets). According to several authors, however, there is significant untapped potential for MNCs in the glocal and local market segments (Khanna and Palepu, 2006; Arnold and Quelch, 1998; Cavusgil et al., 2002; Dawar and Chattopadhay, 2003; Rahman and Bhattacharyya, 2003) or even in the bottom of the pyramid segment (Prahalad and Hammon, 2002; London and Hart, 2004; Kolk and Tulder, 2006).

Strategies in emerging markets

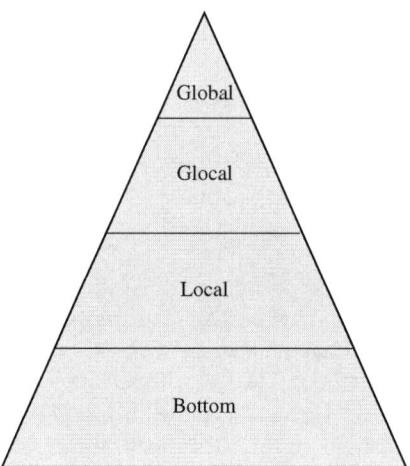

*Figure 1: Market structure of emerging markets
(Source: Khanna and Palepu, 2006)*

Third, as emerging markets often lack segmentation, MNCs may be able to build brand loyalty for a low cost (Dawar and Chattopadhay, 2003; Batra, 1997; Arnold and Quelch, 1998; Meyer and Tran, 2006). However, it is also acknowledged that emerging market customers tend to be less loyal than Western customers.

Finally, as labor costs are relatively low in emerging markets, MNCs may establish sales and marketing infrastructure for far lower cost than in mature markets (Arnold and Quelch, 1998).

The nature of resources

A second distinct dimension of emerging markets is the nature of the resource base, especially the human resource base. The way in which MNCs relate to this resource base can be understood using Michael Porter's value-chain thinking (Porter, 1986). According to this theory, a firm creates value through a value chain consisting of a number of primary and supporting activities. In the process of economic globalization, firms increasingly configure their value chains on an international level by placing value-chain functions in foreign locations. Accordingly, MNCs might disintegrate their value chains and source specific, narrowly defined value-chain functions abroad and maintain others at home. By offshoring specific functions and activities, MNCs may access resources in foreign locations, enhance the efficiency of their existing assets and, in the process, build new advantages (Farrell, 2005). Depending on the relative balance between transaction and coordination costs (Hennart, 1991), offshoring can

Introduction

either take place through movement of production to a controlled subsidiary ("equity based offshoring") or through outsourcing to a local provider ("offshore outsourcing") (Sako, 2005). Stabell and Fjelstad (1998) argue that many firms (e.g., consultant firms, banks or transport firms) should not be described as value chains but rather should be seen as "value shops" or "value networks". These alternative types of value creation logic dissolve the compartmentalized, progressive sequence of value creation activities depicted by value-chain thinking.

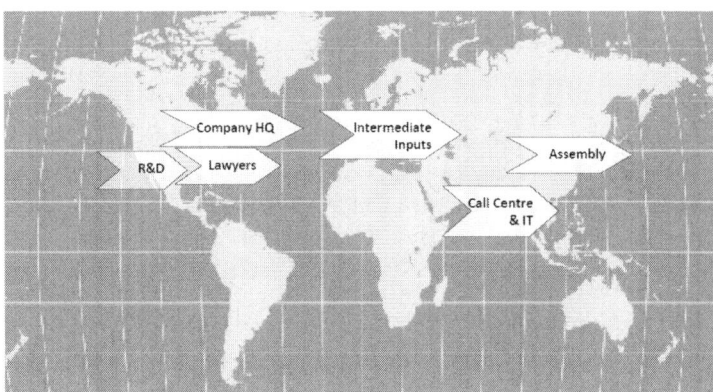

Figure 2: A global value chain configuration

If we look at the offshoring of value-chain functions to emerging markets in particular, the initial and, often, main motive behind offshoring is the MNC's wish to access abundant pools of low-cost labor. Therefore, within the past 10 to 15 years, MNCs have offshored significant amounts of low-value-added and less-advanced functions to emerging markets, such as the production of simple components and mature finished products. More recently, MNCs have offshored the production of relatively standardized types of service tasks, such as routine programming, billing and call center functions (Sako, 2005; Doh, 2005).

However, because emerging markets are fostering growing numbers of highly skilled workers from their own training and educational institutions, because infrastructure is being developed, and because the capabilities of local supplier firms are improving, it has become possible to relocate advanced types of value-chain functions to emerging markets (Scott-Kennel and Enderwick, 2005). Thus, MNCs increasingly offshore activities in order to access skilled labor and talent, as well as world class supply industries (Metters and Verma, 2008). As the offshored functions become more complex, the relationship between the MNCs and the emerging market firm or subsidiary becomes more reciprocal, with mutual learning and development taking place and with strong feedback loops affecting the involved organizations (Dossani and Kenney, 2007; Jensen, 2008).

The quest for skilled human resources in emerging markets inadvertently drives up demand. Salaries for engineers, biochemists, managers and programmers in emerging markets grow at very steep rates. MNCs therefore find themselves in intensifying competition with other MNCs and local firms for talented employees. This puts huge pressure on recruitment and retention practices in MNCs and, accordingly, strategic human resource management becomes a key feature of MNC emerging market strategies (Napier and Vu, 1998; Shen, 2005).

A key role in the integration of emerging markets in global value chains is the role played by shipping and logistics MNCs. Transport costs are often exceptionally high in emerging markets, and inadequate transport infrastructures, such as a lack of land haulage, warehouses and harbors, act as major impediments for MNC sourcing strategies in these countries. In such situations, investments made by shipping and logistics MNCs may play a pivotal role in linking producers in emerging markets with markets in developed countries (Greve et al, 2007).

The nature of institutions

Formal institutions (e.g., rules and regulations, government organizations, business associations) and informal institutions (e.g., networks, customs, conventions, traditions) in emerging markets are often fundamentally different from those in developed countries, which may have profound implications for MNC strategy (see e.g., Hoskisson et al., 2000; Peng, 2002, 2003; Wright et al., 2005; Peng et al., 2008; Kostova et al., 2008). The distinct formal and informal institutions of emerging markets may seriously impair MNC activity in those markets, e.g., by increasing transaction costs (Hoskisson et al, 2000) and/or through increasing the MNCs' "liability of foreignness" (Morisset and Neso, 2002).

Emerging markets will frequently have specific pre-investment and performance measures in place for MNCs. For example, they may require that a certain amount of inputs must be procured locally or only allow MNCs to have a certain degree or percentage of ownership in an activity. Such FDI-related entry and performance measures obviously constrain the strategies that can be pursued by MNCs. Institutions to enforce contracts and intellectual property rights (IPRs; e.g., trademarks and patents) are frequently non-existent, ambiguous, and/or not enforced in emerging markets. In these situations, MNCs need to adjust their strategies accordingly. For instance, they might try to prevent diffusion of IPRs to local competitors by fully internalizing activities (Smarzynska, 1998). In emerging markets, governments typically have a relatively strong hand in the economy, partly as a regulator and partly as a producer. To succeed in such highly governed market contexts, it is particularly important for MNCs to foster good government relations (Luo, 2001). Strong, widespread informal networks among firms in emerging markets often provide highly non-transparent barriers to entry for MNCs, while they offer local firms an advantage over foreign entrants (Khanna and Palepu, 1997).

Finally, emerging market institutions tend to change rapidly and in unpredictable ways. Many emerging markets are in the process of transforming from economies based on relation and network types of market exchange to economies based on Western-style formal, rule-based types of market exchange. Depending on where emerging markets are in such a transition, MNCs need to adjust their strategies to take the dominant mode of exchange into account (Peng, 2003).

A final institutional challenge facing MNCs in emerging markets is related to ethics. Institutional and regulatory voids exist in many emerging markets in terms of labor, environmental, anti-corruption, and human rights legislation and enforcement. Furthermore, there may be differences in the conception of what constitutes "ethical" in developed countries and emerging markets. Therefore, MNCs often face profound uncertainties regarding which modes of conduct are considered ethically correct and acceptable by relevant stakeholders (Jansson, 2007). The response of many MNCs has been to adopt and enforce their own CSR standards, or to adopt and enforce international CSR, environmental and labor norms, such as the Global Compact, ILO rules, ISO 14000, ISO 26000 or the UN's Anti-Corruption Convention (Kolk and Tulder, 2005).

The nature of competition

Many of the factors that shape competition in developed countries assume new meaning when viewed in an emerging market context. First, the payoffs of first-mover strategies may be particularly high given the relatively non-segmented nature of the markets and resource bases, and the sometimes immature nature of local industries. Therefore, MNCs will often embark on aggressive strategies to become first movers or, alternatively, to prevent their competitors from attaining a first-mover advantage (Aussilloux, 2000). As a consequence, one may witness a virtual "herding" behavior, where MNCs encroach on an emerging market location, often with little consideration of the realistic payoffs from the entry (Lung, 2000; Hoenen and Hansen, 2009).

While the potential first-mover advantages in emerging markets might be very large, the risks are also high: The market may not be ready for the MNCs' products, the costs of developing the market could be too high, or the local supply industry might be incapable of meeting MNC requirements in terms of quality and delivery times. Therefore, some MNCs may profit from letting their competitors carry the costs of market and resource development, and only moving in when the market and the resource base are ripe (Ramamurti, 2000).

More generally, it appears that the largest emerging markets are becoming battlegrounds for fierce consolidation games in oligopolistic industries, such as cement production, windmills, electronics and breweries. In some of these industries, emerging markets are the last remaining major markets still "up for grabs". Therefore, large MNCs converge on these markets to build dominant positions, sometimes through greenfield investments, but mainly through mergers and acquisitions (Schenk, 1999). Incidentally, MNCs in oligopolistic industries are not only motivated to move into emerging markets by the actual or potential moves of peers. An additional, increasingly important competitive consideration is the fact that new, powerful competitors are arising from within these countries, threatening the positions of developed country MNCs (Hobday, 1995; Ramamurti and Singh, 2009; Mathews, 2006). Therefore, MNCs increasingly invest in emerging markets to "quell" or "check" rising emerging market firms (Nielsen, 2005; Hoenen and Hansen, 2009).

How the cases illustrate challenges and opportunities in emerging markets

All of the emerging market characteristics mentioned above have - to a higher or lesser degree - affected the strategies of the case MNCs. Some of the cases illustrate how firms relate to the particular market characteristics of emerging markets. For instance, we learn how companies like Carlsberg and Bestseller in consumer markets, and Danfoss in BtB markets have built market positions in China that are so strong that these positions have become key to these companies' global portfolios. Surprisingly good market performance in India has been instrumental in creating a strong position for the local subsidiary of FLSmidth, and has helped the subsidiary build a regional and global mandate. A.P. Møller – Mærsk succeeded in carving out a dominant position in BtB markets for transport and logistics by being present in Vietnam at an early stage. The Bestseller case vividly illustrates how adaptation of products and marketing to local market conditions can generate significant value. The case also illustrates how a company can build a strong brand quickly and at a relatively low cost in an emerging market.

In terms of access to resources, it is demonstrated that several of the companies have invested in India and China to gain access to low-cost labor. ECCO has a long history of moving production to low-cost countries, a process that eventually led ECCO to China. Even among the market seekers, several are focusing on cost reduction through local sourcing in order to stay or become competitive in local markets. For instance, Vestas aims to source 80% of its inputs from Indian suppliers in order to enhance competitiveness in the Indian market and other emerging markets. Other case companies undertake advanced types of resource-seeking in India and China. FLSmidth was originally a market seeker in India but "discovered" the huge Indian sourcing potential in terms of

Introduction

engineering services, which led to it having almost 3,000, mainly, engineers in the country. The Vestas and Danfoss cases document how these companies are contemplating the placement of highly advanced activities, such as R&D functions, in India and China, respectively.

A.P. Møller – Mærsk plays a key role in the offshoring undertaken by other MNCs. By providing transport and logistics services in countries that were previously weak on such services, A.P. Møller – Mærsk opens such countries up to MNC sourcing operations. Therefore, A.P. Møller – Mærsk is a typical network type of firm (Stabell and Fjelstad, 1998), bringing local and foreign firms in Vietnam and MNCs in the north together by providing sophisticated shipping and logistics services.

In terms of institutions, several of the case companies have tried to guard themselves against instable or absent institutions by internalizing activities. Vestas, for instance, originally entered India through a joint venture, partly because Indian FDI regulation required local ownership, partly because a joint venture partnership eased the interaction with Indian authorities. However, Vestas became increasingly concerned with the way in which the local partner conducted the business (e.g., overselling the product, focusing too much on government subsidies and failing to provide adequate after-sale services). Eventually, as the Indian Government eased requirements to local ownership, Vestas reconfigured its Indian business as a wholly owned operation. ECCO attempted to reduce uncertainty related to trade regimes by diversifying its portfolio among several Asian countries – a prudent move in light of the recent trade dispute between China and the EU over the shoe trade. The importance of good government relations in emerging markets is illustrated by several cases: A.P. Møller – Mærsk was present in Vietnam at an early stage and worked to ensure close relations with the Vietnamese government, which in turn rewarded A.P. Møller – Mærsk with the task of building a large harbor in southern Vietnam. This case also illustrates how A.P. Møller – Mærsk, given the exceptionally high asset specificity of its investment in Vietnam, is now highly dependent on the Vietnamese government. The ethical issues in emerging markets are also evident in several of the cases. For instance, the ECCO case illustrates how ensuring a high environmental standard was key to obtaining a license to operate a tannery in China.

In terms of competition, several cases illustrate how rivalry in global oligopolistic industries has moved into emerging markets in earnest, and how this rivalry may be particularly intense due to the relatively non-segmented nature of markets here. For instance, Carlsberg failed to build a market position in eastern China due to the intense competition but it then moved toward the "unchartered" western China markets, where it succeeded in building a dominant market position. While there were conventional market-and resource-based considerations behind Danfoss's engagement in China, one important motivation was to keep

Strategies in emerging markets

an eye on up-and-coming rival firms from China. In general, many of the cases illustrate the growing challenge posed by firms coming from *within* China and India.

	Special factors affecting business in emerging markets		
	Emerging market (EM) characteristic	*Implications for MNCs*	*Indicative cases*
Markets	Rapid market growth	A growing share of many MNCs' market portfolios will be in EMs	Bestseller, Carlsberg, Danfoss, APM, Vestas, ECCO, FLSmidth
	Market structure consists of global, glocal, local and BOP markets	MNCs may not only focus on global market segment but also on local market segments	Bestseller, Carlsberg, Danfoss
	Low levels of market segmentation	Opportunities to build brand loyalty and marketing infrastructure at a low cost	Bestseller, Carlsberg
Resources	Abundant low-cost labor	Opportunities for global sourcing of standardized tasks	FLSmidth, ECCO
	Growing competencies of local resource base	Opportunities to tap into knowledge and recruit global talent	FLSmidth, Vestas
	Growing competition for labor	Employee and partner retention is a key competition parameter	FLSmidth
	Problems of integrating into global value chains	Offer high-quality logistics and transport services	APM
Institutions	Volatile and uncertain institutional environment	Use networks/joint ventures/alliances to circumvent lack of formal institutions; internalize activities to curb opportunism	ECCO, Vestas
	The state plays a very active role in the economy	Good connections to local authorities are imperative	ECCO, APM, Vestas
	Weak IPR regimes	MNCs have to proactively enforce their IPR and/or fully internalize activities in order to appropriate rents from IPR	ECCO, Danfoss, Vestas
	Ethical uncertainty	MNCs have to prove/document/elicit corporate social responsibility	ECCO
Competition	Opportunities for significant first-mover advantages at a low cost	Need to balance costs and benefits of accessing consumer and resource markets before competitors	Carlsberg, Bestseller, Vestas
	Rising EM competitors challenging western incumbents	Need to check/quell upcoming EM competitors	Danfoss, Bestseller, Vestas

Conclusion

Danish MNCs' investments in China and India used to play minor roles in the overall strategies of the parent companies, as these countries mainly hosted relatively insignificant market portfolios or provided standardized, commoditized inputs that could easily be substituted with inputs obtained elsewhere. However, the seven cases presented in this book confirm that these countries have become crucial to the overall strategies of Danish MNCs, either as vital market portfolios or as locations for key value-chain functions, or both. For Carlsberg, the emerging market strategy arguably became paramount to its survival as a market leader– western China was an important component of this strategy. For FLSmidth, the offshoring of engineering services to India was key to its movement toward a more cost-effective and focused business platform. China became one of the largest markets in Bestseller's portfolio, while for ECCO, the massive investment in Chinese factories meant that a large portion of its global production was moved to China. In essence, the future fate of all of these companies appears to be increasingly linked to India and China

Another general message evident in the case studies is that the road taken by emerging markets subsidiaries to obtain key roles in the strategies of their parent companies has been far from straight. In several cases, China and India appear to have gained importance largely by coincidence and in unanticipated ways. FLSmidth India started as a joint venture aimed at the local Indian market. Only a radical change of strategy at the Danish headquarters, combined with a huge Indian market expansion, and manpower shortages in Denmark and the US, made it possible for the Indian subsidiary to obtain a global sourcing mandate. Bestseller entered China through a small joint venture detached from the main organization. The joint venture was partly aimed at exploring market opportunities and partly designed to improve Bestseller's Chinese sourcing activity. Only after a few years of operation was the full potential of a dedicated market focus in China realized, which put Bestseller on a path that meant the Chinese operation would eventually grow to several thousand outlets. Moreover, the road to success in China and India for the case companies was far from uninterrupted. For instance, Carlsberg stumbled in its early China entry by focusing on the eastern Chinese markets and on premium beer. Having lost the game in the east, Carlsberg turned west, moving into large tracts of the beer markets in that region before the competition could react.

In the coming years, many Danish firms will try their luck in India and China. Some will fail, while others will succeed. Some will be able to plan the outcomes and others will see their investments move in directions they never anticipated. In either case, we hope that this collection of cases may help managers as well as students of strategy in emerging markets see the massive potential in doing business in the two Asian giants, and assist them in understanding the challenges inherent in such an endeavor.

CHAPTER 2

Carlsberg A/S – Probably the best beer company in western China

A breeze of optimism blew through the office of Carlsberg A/S's CEO, Jørgen Buhl Rasmussen. After finally gaining 100% control over the giant Russian brewery, Baltic Beverages Holding (BBH), and with the investments in western China beginning to bear fruit, the newly appointed CEO was confident that the Danish brewing company's intensified focus on emerging markets would pay off. The company was counting on tapping the massive potential in emerging markets in order to achieve a much-needed reduction in its dependency on the maturing and stagnating west European beer markets, which accounted for a full 61% of the company's revenue in 2007.

Indeed, Carlsberg's emerging market efforts had come a long way. In the Russian market, which was considered to be one of the fastest-growing beer markets in the world, Carlsberg enjoyed market-leader status through its ownership of BBH. In that market, it had a sales volume of approximately 23 million hectoliters of beer in 2007 and revenue of DKK 9.0 billion (USD 1.8 billion). As for the highly promising Chinese market, which was regarded as the world's largest beer market in terms of population and size, the Danish company had achieved a 55% market share in the western parts of the country, and it operated 20 brewery plants in China with close to 5,000 employees. In fact, as Carlsberg recognized that the European markets would eventually reach a point of saturation, the aim of the Chinese investments was to create a platform for future growth and revenue.

The outlook for Carlsberg had not always been as bright as it appeared by 2008. Carlsberg's emerging market strategy had taken a long and winding road. For instance, Carlsberg's acquisition of the BBH shares was the result of a troubled and expensive partnership with Norwegian Orkla ASA. In addition, before Carlsberg had become successful in the western provinces of China, the company had spent plenty of valuable time and resources trying to enter the rich provinces of southeastern China, a strategy that had failed. Furthermore, in the early 2000s, Carlsberg was on the brink of being reduced to a secondary player in the global beer market – as the consolidation of the industry proceeded, Carlsberg A/S became an obvious takeover target and was also at risk of being cornered as a small regional player. Nonetheless, as the first decade of the millennium neared an end, Carlsberg was the fifth-largest brewery in the world in terms of volumes produced. Much of this reversal of fortune could be attributed to the company's emerging market focus.

Despite Buhl Rasmussen's optimism about the future, the real question was how Carlsberg A/S could successfully continue to capitalize on its growing engagement in emerging markets. "We don't know how large the Chinese market will be in five years, and I don't know if China can become a new BBH", the CEO explained, "but it is definitely not impossible, as the market is enormous".[3] It was no surprise that competition was becoming increasingly fierce in this booming emerging market, and history had clearly proven that doing business successfully in this market required unconventional approaches.

Introducing Carlsberg A/S

The successful course and strategy which Carlsberg has pursued in recent years will remain basically the same no matter what. The strategy has proved its worth with growth and better results, and it is now strongly rooted in our organisation. Our business is thus to focus on the beer markets in Western Europe, Eastern Europe and Asia.

Carlsberg A/S CEO, Jørgen Buhl Rasmussen[4]

As the fifth-largest brewing company in the world, Carlsberg A/S's vision was "our brands will be the consumer's first choice, and we will lead our industry in profitability and growth through a culture of quality, innovation and continuous improvement". Moreover, Carlsberg saw itself as "probably the best beer company in the world".[5]

The core businesses of Carlsberg A/S were brewing, marketing and selling beer. In 1847, J.C. Jacobsen opened the doors of Carlsberg A/S's first brewery in Copenhagen, Denmark, and the first foreign brewery was established in Malawi in 1968. In 2007, the company had 33,000 employees, held a portfolio of 75 breweries around the world and sold approximately 115 million hectoliters of beer in more than 150 countries, with net revenue of DKK 44,750 million (EUR 6,000 million) (see Exhibit 1). Carlsberg's areas of operation focused on the mature beer markets of Western Europe, the growth markets of Eastern Europe and the emerging Asian markets. Behind this strong position of the company was a major reorientation and restructuring of the company of recent years: "Progress in revenue and share prices has been driven by a fundamental revolution of the company", explained former CEO Nils Smedegaard Andersen. "We have purchased and then professionalized the business. At the same time, we have worked with the structure."[6]

Organization

Despite Carlsberg's position as the fifth-largest brewery in the world by 2008 (see Exhibits 2 and 3), at the beginning of the 2000s, it had found itself largely excluded from the league of large international breweries. Carlsberg, it then seemed, was losing ground as one of the strongest brands in the world, and was considered by analysts to be an obvious takeover target for larger breweries. In an attempt to cope with these difficulties, a merger with Norwegian Orkla ASA's brewing activities was executed in 2000 and resulted in the creation of Carlsberg Breweries. Carlsberg A/S owned 60% of the new entity, while Orkla held 40%. Among the positive aspects of this merger was Orkla ASA's 50% ownership in Baltic Beverages Holdings (BBH), which offered Carlsberg the possibility to strengthen its position in the East European markets. However, after a number of strategic disagreements, Carlsberg bought Orkla out of the merger in 2004. Although this move put Carlsberg into severe debt, former CEO Nils Smedegaard Andersen was content: "We are market leaders in a handful of large countries, we own half of the largest brewery in Eastern Europe and we possess a majority share in a number of European breweries". He also emphasized that "the acquisition of Orkla's Carlsberg shares, as well as Holsten, prove that, during the last five years, we have reached a size and economic capacity that allow us to invest very large sums of money".[7]

In retrospect, Carlsberg's ownership structure was a main contributor to the difficulties of financing expansion. The largest shareholder of Carlsberg A/S was the Carlsberg Foundation, which was established by J.C. Jacobsen in 1876 with the purpose of funding scientific research and social work. The Foundation was obliged to own at least 51% of Carlsberg A/S's shares, which hindered the quick release of capital for acquisitions and blocked potential fusions with large, foreign breweries. This was a serious disadvantage for an international brewery fighting to be among the top players in a rapidly consolidating industry.

Carlsberg A/S appeared unable to secure continuous growth and development, and many feared that the company would become a superfluous player. However, after the buyout of Orkla ASA, Carlsberg's management started to look forward. As Povl Krogsgaard-Larsen, the Carlsberg Foundation's Chairman, pointed out, "we then began to prepare ourselves for our next move, namely to change the charter of the Foundation. This would give Carlsberg more freedom to act, as the Foundation was locked in terms of capital after we bought Orkla's shares back".[8] As a result of this process, the Foundation was obligated to own only 25% of Carlsberg A/S shares after May 2007, which created more room for new capital.

Strategies in emerging markets

In May 2008, Carlsberg, in cooperation with Heineken, completed a DKK 104 billion (USD 22 billion) acquisition of the largest British brewer, Scottish & Newcastle. This acquisition gave Heineken control over Scottish & Newcastle's British activities, while Carlsberg obtained the remaining 50% of the Russian brewery, Baltic Beverages Holding. Naturally, this major acquisition increased Carlsberg's debt, which reached DKK 58.3 billion in May 2008 (USD 12.1 billion).

Towards an emerging market strategy

With global beer brands such as Carlsberg Pilsner (*Probably the best beer in world*), regional brands such as Tuborg, Holsten and Baltika, and a number of leading local brands, Carlsberg's most important markets were in Western Europe, which accounted for 61% of revenue in 2007. Furthermore, the company held a strong position in the growth markets of Eastern Europe and in the emerging Asian markets, with Russia and China serving as the most notable examples. The booming Indian market was also regarded as a market of increasing importance. The East European and Asian markets accounted for 33% and 6% of revenue in 2007, respectively (see Exhibit 3).

The global brewing industry of the mid 2000s was characterized by a process of intense consolidation, in which the number of breweries continuously declined. By 2007, the industry was basically controlled by the five largest breweries in the world (see Exhibit 4). This consolidation process could be ascribed to changes in consumers' beer-drinking habits as well as increasing production costs. In the mature European and American markets, beer consumption had been falling as a result of growing health consciousness and increased competition from wine and spirits, while the East European and Asian beer markets were booming. Given the rising costs of inputs, such as glass, aluminum and hops, the large breweries were seeking to consolidate and increase their market shares as they searched for economies of scales in relation to everything from production to advertisement. For the consolidation of foreign markets, acquisitions and joint ventures with local firms were the preferred modes of entry for the largest companies in the beer industry, as they allowed acquiring companies to gain access to local brands, distributional networks and local market knowledge through partnerships with local breweries.

As markets around the world became increasingly consolidated, Carlsberg recognized its inability to become a truly global company. The North and South American markets had been lost to other well-known, established breweries, and the potential offered by the African markets was of limited interest. The west European markets were already consolidated to a great extent, so Carlsberg decided to focus on Eastern Europe and Asia as a means of achieving future growth. Investments in these emerging markets were financed through revenues

Carlsberg A/S

from activities in the west European markets. Carlsberg's activities in Eastern Europe, particularly in Russia, were expected to offer sizeable potential for several years. However, expectations were, perhaps, even greater for the long-term potential of the Asian markets, especially China, where Carlsberg was making considerable investments. In fact, Carlsberg's emerging market focus was considered vital for the company's ability to remain a major player in the beer industry. "We want to ensure that we have positions with future growth potential, and we will be relatively patient," former CEO Nils Smedegaard Andersen argued in 2005. "We are unable to say anything about how long it will take, but right now we believe that a market-leading position will be interesting in five to ten years. How interesting will depend on the competition, the economic development and many other conditions".[9] The increase in optimism concerning Carlsberg's future was, therefore, due in large part to the fact that the company had abandoned its strategy of becoming a global player and instead focused on capitalizing on emerging markets.

Central to Carlsberg's business strategy was a focus on value creation and profitable growth. The west European strategy was to ensure "improved profitability through innovation and streamlining", while "rapid growth and higher earnings" were emphasized in Eastern Europe. The Asian strategy was "long-term growth through building up market positions" (see Exhibit 5).[10]

The beer industry's mantra, according to Heineken CEO Jean-Francois van Boxmeer, was that it was not worthwhile for a brewing company to be present in a market where it was not the market leader or the runner-up. This philosophy was shared by Carlsberg, as indicated by Carlsberg's Press Officer, Jens Peter Skaarup: "What is important is the position we have on the markets in which we are present." In relation to the consolidation of the industry, he argued that "competition is something we are happy about. It makes us more 'fit for fight'". [11]

Carlsberg in Russia

Once Carlsberg gained access to BBH through the Orkla ASA merger, the scene was set for Carlsberg to reap the major benefits of the emerging East European markets. In 2007, when Carlsberg owned 50% of BBH's shares, the Russian brewery held a market share of 37.6% in Russia and was the market leader. BBH operations in Eastern Europe – Russia, the Ukraine, the Baltic states, Kazakhstan, Uzbekistan and Belarus – accounted for 23% of Carlsberg's revenue in 2007. The Russian market was undoubtedly the most important for BBH, as it represented 79% of sales volumes and 86% of operating profit. From 2006 to 2007, the Russian market grew by 16%, while annual beer consumption per capita amounted to 75 liters (the average was in the Scandinavian markets 65 liters). This positive development was expected to continue in Russia in the coming years, as vodka consumption was declining due to new taxes on liquor, which increased the price of vodka. In fact, the Russian market was considered to be one of the fastest-growing beer markets in the world.

Carlsberg's strategy in terms of BBH and the Russian market was to grow organically by capturing new market shares. The company doubted that the Russian state would accept more acquisitions by a company who was the absolute market leader. However, for Christian Ramm-Schmidt, BBH's CEO, organic growth was not a problem: "I cannot see why that should not be possible. BBH is a national company, and it has the best brands, the best distribution and strong management. That should suffice to capture 1 to 2 percentage points a year".[12] In order to support this strategy, Carlsberg invested in BBH's production capacity, infrastructure and logistics, as well as in the building of strong brands through product development and advertising.

BBH's best-selling brand was Baltika, "a foamy, golden brew with a delicate flavour of hops and the aroma of first-class malt".[13] It also was Russia's leading brand with a market share of 38% in 2007. In order to reduce Carlsberg's dependency on the Russian market, the company had great expectations for Baltika on an international scale, and planned to introduce the brand in Asia and the US. "I can see possibilities for Baltika in most parts of the world," explained Jørgen Buhl Rasmussen. "Just like you can sell Czech beer almost everywhere today, I believe the same could happen for a brand like Baltika."[14] Furthermore, Buhl Rasmussen did not believe that introducing Baltika in other markets would have negative effects on Carlsberg's other brands: "We do not see any risk at all of cannibalizing our own brands".[15] BBH also distributed Carlsberg Pilsner and Tuborg brands to the Russian market, where the aim was to capture the premium segments. In fact, the Tuborg brand was BBH's most important international brand, as it represented 11% of revenue in 2007. The Carlsberg Pilsner brand accounted for 2% of revenue in the same year.

However, as the Russian market was attractive, Carlsberg was not the only international brewing company interested in capturing market shares as the west European and American markets began to stagnate. Heineken acquired five breweries in Russia in 2005 and was the third-largest beer company on the Russian market in terms of volume by 2007. In addition, Heineken was selling local brands, such as Volga and Ochata. South African/British SABMiller was also active on the Russian market with a 6% market share and it was planning to acquire more Russian breweries.

Carlsberg in China

Carlsberg's history in China spanned as far back as the late 1890s when the first barrels of beer were exported from Denmark. It was, however, not until 1981 – when Carlsberg Brewery Hong Kong was established – that Carlsberg began to produce beer in China. The Chinese market was considered highly important for Carlsberg, even though the yearly per capita consumption of beer was just 29 liters in 2007. Given its vast size and high population, China was the world's largest market in terms of production and consumption, and the market's estimated growth rate was up to 8% per year, compared to 0.7% in the US and 2.5% in Europe. In other words, the market was not to be underestimated.

The Chinese beer market was immensely fragmented and highly regionalized with no truly national brewery. Local and regional non-premium brands dominated and price was often the determinant factor. These types of beer constituted more than 95% of total beer sales. In addition, entry barriers were considered to be very high, and the industry was capital intensive in terms of production and distribution. In order to be profitable, it was necessary to be either number one or number two. For that reason, competition had led to a process of consolidation, where the large international breweries mainly competed on buying shares of regional and local breweries.

Following initial setbacks, which led to a complete overhaul of the original strategy, Carlsberg was positioned somewhat differently from its competitors in the competition for the Chinese market. In 2000, Carlsberg had entered into a 50/50 joint venture with the Thai company Chang Beverages Pte Ltd – a leading player in Asian markets for alcoholic beverages – and created Carlsberg Asia Ltd. (CAL) to strengthen Carlsberg's position on the Asian markets. In the important southeastern Chinese market, however, CAL met fierce competition, and earnings and sales did not take off as expected. In 2003, Anheuser-Busch, SAB-Miller, Interbrew and Heineken together held a substantial proportion of shares in China's four largest breweries, and controlled more than 30% of the Chinese beer market in collaboration with their partners. Furthermore, as time passed, disagreements between Carlsberg and Chang Beverages arose, which eventually led to Carlsberg pulling out of the joint venture in 2003. However, as this move was allegedly a violation of the contract between the two partners, Carlsberg was forced to pay compensation of DKK 734 million. As a result of this episode, Carlsberg not only experienced severe financial losses but also lost three strategically important years in which to establish itself in the Chinese and Asian beer markets. During these years, other international competitors acquired important market shares in the southeast Chinese beer market, while Carlsberg, with its assets first tied up in Thailand and later finding itself financially strained from the lawsuit, was unable to muster the financial strength needed to acquire new production facilities and enter the competition.

This significant setback inhibited Carlsberg from taking part in the initial consolidation process in southeast China, which caused the company to revise its strategy for Asia and the Chinese market. The result was a focus on the highly fragmented, poor western Chinese provinces. "Our strategy is to pursue the provinces in the west, as we can buy cheap and because it is a foundation for

Strategies in emerging markets

growth," explained Carlsberg's Information Officer, Margrete Skov. "The good forecasts for growth are a result of China's 'go west' policy with large investments in the provinces in the west. That gives a larger economy and better sale opportunities", she continued.[16]

The cornerstone of Carlsberg's new strategy was a focus on achieving leadership and first-mover advantages in western China, while avoiding the fierce competition in the southeast. Geographically, the west Chinese region included five provinces, which covered one-third of China and had a population of around 100 million. The western regions were the poorest parts of China, and the living standards and the level of beer consumption were lower than the country average. In the western province of Yunnan, for instance, yearly beer consumption per capita only amounted to 4 liters, in contrast to 70-90 liters in the big eastern cities.

Nevertheless, Carlsberg expected living standards and beer consumption to rise rapidly. According to Michael Fredskov Christiansen, Director of the Chinese operations, it was crucial for the company to be present in western China when growth accelerated. He expected Carlsberg's turnover to rise in line with the general growth in the Chinese beer market.[17] In addition, the western Chinese market was more fragmented, and none of the other large players were present, as they all concentrated on the southeast. Carlsberg's 2007 Annual Report 2007 indicated that the company's strategy was "to build up a leading position in these emerging markets through acquisitions and subsequent strong organic growth, so that Asia makes a greater contribution to Carlsberg's overall earnings in the future".[18]

In 2007, Carlsberg had operations in 20 brewery plants and 4,756 employees in China. Only a handful of the Chinese breweries were fully owned by Carlsberg, while the rest were operated through joint ventures with local partners, the Danish Industrialization Fund for Developing Countries (IFU) and local authorities. These efforts gave Carlsberg an overall market share of approximately 55-60% in western China, making it the only international brewery with a leading position in that region. In addition to selling local brands, Carlsberg experienced increasing success with Carlsberg Chill, a brand designed for the Chinese market. This beer targeted the more exclusive segments and was distributed not only in western China but also in the east. In this respect, Jørgen Buhl Rasmussen argued, "we are interested in approaching nearby areas by continuously moving from the west towards central China – for instance through acquisitions". However, he also stated that "alone in western China, the possibilities are enormous. We control approximately 60% of [the] western China [beer market] in an area of a population of approximately 120 million. That is far more than Great Britain and Scandinavia together, and it is a market where the consumers continuously buy better, more expensive beer".[19]

Even though the Asian investments had yet to show their full potential, former CEO Niels Smedegaard Andersen emphasized that "we are in China to create a position. And we are not counting on making money in perhaps five to ten years. Carlsberg has to establish new markets." He also argued that "we consider western Europe to be a mature, stagnating market. Russia and Eastern Europe are growth markets, while Asia is a developing market".[20]

* * *

Considering Carlsberg's activities in emerging markets, CEO Jørgen Buhl Rasmussen was optimistic. He was convinced that the company's timely and successful emerging market strategy and positioning had ensured that Carlsberg was prepared to successfully capitalize on its investments in the emerging economies. However, Rasmussen was fully aware that the majority of the company's revenue was still generated in the stagnating Western European markets and that new sources of revenue were needed. At the same time, the BBH success story was likely to soon be affected by ever-fiercer competition, and the Russian government was contemplating worrisome taxation proposals for alcohol in general and beer in particular, which could seriously challenge the profitability of Carlsberg's Russian operations. Moreover, despite magnificent forecasts for the Asian markets, the annual consumption per capita was still humble and had yet to take off.

Therefore, Carlsberg's shareholders would need time and patience if they wished to see whether Carlsberg's emerging market strategy would suffice as a response to the operational, competitive and regulatory challenges that these markets posed. In the longer term, the payoff could be significant.

Exhibits for Carlsberg A/S case

Exhibit 1 – Carlsberg A/S key figures[21]

	2003	2004	2005	2006	2007
Sales volume (million hl)					
Beer	81.4	92.0	101.6	100.7	115.2
Soft drinks	21.2	19.4	19.1	20.2	20.8
Profit and loss account (DKK million)					
Net revenue	34,626	36,284	38,047	41,083	44,750
Profit before taxation	2,688	1,651	1,892	3,029	3,634
Profit for the year	1,719	1,269	1,371	2,171	2,596
Balance sheet total	46,712	57,698	62,359	58,451	61,220
Equity	11,276	15,084	17,968	17,597	18,621
Net interest-bearing debt	8,929	21,733	20,753	19,229	19,726
Key ratios					
Operating margin, %	10.3	9.4	9.2	9.8	11.8
ROIC, %	12.4	8.1	7.8	9.2	11.7
Equity ratio, %	38.3	29.1	31.3	32.5	32.6
Debt/equity (financial gearing), X	0.50	1.29	1.06	1.01	0.99
Employees	31,531	31,703	30,208	31,680	33,420

Exhibit 2 – The global beer industry, 2007[22]

	Largest breweries	Sales volume (mill. hl.)
1	InBev	271.0
2	SABMiller	239.0
3	Anheuser-Busch	128.4
4	Heineken	119.8
5	Carlsberg	115.2

Strategies in emerging markets

Exhibit 3 – Carlsberg A/S global markets, 2007[23]

	Beer consumption per capita (L/year)	Market position	Market share (%)	Employees	Breweries	Invested capital (DKK million)	Beer sales pro rata (million hl)	Revenue (DKK million)	Operating margin (%)	ROIC (%)
Western Europe						16,152	28.5	27,944	2,738	16.0
Denmark	83	1	64	2,332	2					
Norway	59	1	52	1,554	3					
Sweden	52	1	38	1,152	1					
Finland	87	1	50	1,003	2					
UK	91	4	13	2,060	2					
Germany	115	1		1,449	4					
Switzerland	59	1	41	1,453	2					
Italy	32	3	6	802	1					
Portugal	64	1	52	892	2					
Eastern Europe (BBH)				8,174		8,987	29.1	10,435	2,338	29.1
Russia	75	1	38		10					
Ukraine	58	3	20		3					
Baltic states	67-98	1	45		4					
Kazakhstan	34	1	23		1					
Uzbekistan	11	2	25		2					
Eastern Europe (excl. BBH)						4,248	14.8	4,267	477	11.3
Poland	88	3	13	1,319	3					
Southeast Europe	64-84	2-3	15-23	1,336	4					
Turkey	11	2	15	564	1					
Asia						3,033	9.6	2,535	330	11.5
Malaysia	5	2	44	596	1					
Singapore	19	2	23	67						
Vietnam	17	4	10	570	2					
China (western China)	29 (15)	(1)	(55)	4,754	20					
Other countries	n.a.	n.a.	n.a.	n.a.	5					

Carlsberg A/S

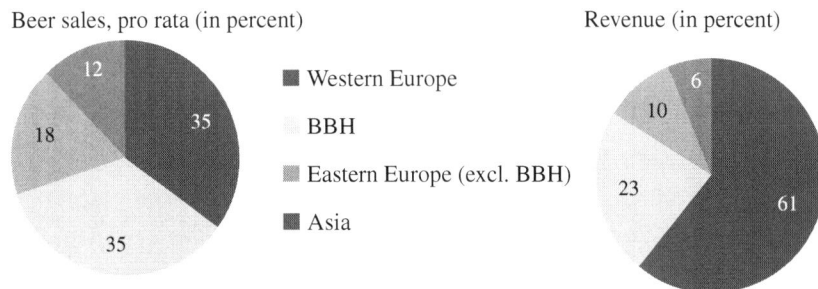

Strategies in emerging markets

Exhibit 4 – Carlsberg's competitors

InBev

	2003	2004	2005	2006	2007
Sales volume (mill. hl.)	108	162	224	247	271
Net revenue (mill EUR)	7,004	8,568	11,656	13,308	14,430
Net profit (mill EUR)	505	719	904	1,411	2,198
Worldwide beer volume 2007, %					
North America	4,60				
Latin America North	37,30				
Latin America South	11,30				
Western Europe	13,30				
Central and Eastern Europe	18,20				
Asia Pacific	13,40				
Global Export and Holding Companies	1,90				

Famous brands: Stella Artois, Bech's, Hoegaarden, Leffe, Staropramen

Anheuser-Busch

	2003	2004	2005	2006	2007
Sales volume (mill. hl.)	110	117	122	125	128
Net revenue (mill EUR)	9,151	9,660	9,726	10,166	10,793
Net profit (mill EUR)	1,343	1,449	1,190	1,271	1,368
Worldwide beer volume 2007, %					
U.S.	81,30				
International	18,70				

Famous brands: Budweiser, Michelob

Heineken

	2003	2004	2005	2006	2007
Sales volume (mill. hl.)	85	97	101	112	120
Net revenue (mill EUR)	9,255	10,062	10,796	11,829	12,654
Net profit (mill EUR)	798	642	761	807	1,211
Worldwide beer volume 2007, %					
Western Europe	30,40				
Central and Eastern Europe	10,50				
Americas	36,80				
Africa and the Middle East	6,50				
Asia Pacific	15,80				

Famous brands: Heineken, Amstel

SABMiller

	2003	2004	2005	2006	2007
Sales volume (mill. hl.)	n.a.	n.a.	n.a.	n.a.	239
Net revenue (mill EUR)	8,179	9,407	11,048	13,354	15,412
Net profit (mill EUR)	417	984	931	1,067	1,309
Worldwide beer volume 2007, %					
Latin America	25				
Europe	20				
North America	10				
Africa and Asia	12				
South Africa	33				

Famous brands: Pilsner, Urquell, Peroni Nastro Azzurro, Grolsch, Carling's Black Label

Exhibit 5 – Carlsberg A/S regional strategies[24]

	Western Europe	BBH and the rest of Eastern Europe	Asia
Strategy	Improved profitability through innovation and streamlining	Rapid growth and higher earnings	Long-term growth through build-up of market positions
Group focus	• Innovation • Marketing and brand building • Continuous streamlining • Corporate culture and management development		
Regional focus	• Maintaining and developing market positions • Marketing • Innovation • Focus on value • Streamlining on every level	• Strengthening and developing market positions • Increased focus on premium segments • Investments • Optimization	• Strengthening the product range • Improving sales work • Strengthening existing market positions through organic growth • Establishing new market positions through acquisitions

43

CHAPTER 3

ECCO A/S – Producing the Dragon's footwear

Morten Bay Jensen, the Managing Director of ECCO Xiamen Co. Ltd, was enjoying his view from the banks of the Jiulong River in Xiamen, China on a November afternoon in 2008. As he thought about how many vessels went in and out of this special economic zone every day, Bay Jensen gazed across the river towards ECCO's new full-scale production site. In a matter of only four years, the Danish footwear company had succeeded in erecting not only five production facilities, which produced 900,000 shoes in 2008, but also a brand new tannery, which was the largest investment in ECCO's history and one of the world's most energy-efficient, environmentally-friendly leather production facilities. With 3,210 employees under his command, he knew that this production site could eventually play a central role in ECCO's business strategy.

A global producer of shoes, ECCO had a highly impressive business record with years of solid double-digit growth. However, it was facing mounting challenges. Not only had the consolidated growth in revenue fallen from 17% in 2007 to a mere 5% in 2008, but the company was also losing significance in its largest markets, Western Europe and North America. ECCO had recently cut 1,200 employees from its global labor force of 16,000 as a result of a falling customer demand. The opportunity to further supplement and optimize the global value chain through the Chinese activities was, therefore, of crucial importance to the company.

Although Bay Jensen was proud of his achievements, he found some matters increasingly troubling. First, as a result of ECCO's "from cow to customer" philosophy, most of the Chinese activities were deliberately kept internally. In this way, ECCO aimed to maximize the productivity and quality of the entire shoe production. However, Bay Jensen knew that this setup might imply certain disadvantages and that it was against the industry norm – competitors, such as Timberland and Geox, were outsourcing most of their production.

Second, the pressure to keep costs down was accelerating in the footwear industry. During its roughly 40-year history, ECCO had proactively offshored its

Strategies in emerging markets

production to low-cost countries: to Portugal in 1984, Indonesia in 1991, Thailand in 1993, Slovakia in 1998 and, eventually, to China in 2005. However, costs in China, particularly in terms of staff, rents and marketing, were on the rise due to increasing competition for resources. As times were changing, an increasing number of shoe manufacturers were moving production to lower-cost countries like Vietnam and Cambodia. ECCO, therefore, needed to consider whether it should find even cheaper production locations and how such an undertaking would influence the quality of the finished shoe – an issue highly central to ECCO's philosophy.

Lastly, the challenges related to the Chinese business environment were staggering. In addition to the cost factors, piracy was a constant challenge – Chinese shoe producers were plagiarizing and abusing ECCO's well-known brand. Furthermore, the newly introduced EU tariffs on shoes exported from China impeded the full utilization of the Chinese production facilities.

As the dark clouds gathered on the horizon over the Pacific Ocean, Bay Jensen knew that the rain was coming and that he had to find some shelter. At this time of year, a downpour could start in a matter of seconds, almost without warning. While finding shelter would save him from getting soaked, it would also give him the opportunity to consider how best to analyze how his business division could function in the most competitive way.

Introducing ECCO A/S

ECCO's vision was to be "the most wanted brand within innovation and comfort footwear – a position that only can be attained by constantly and courageously researching new paths, investing in employees, in our core competencies of product development and production technology".[25] The company was founded by Karl Toosbuy as a family owned enterprise in 1963 in the rural village of Bredebro, Denmark. The original slogan, "A perfect fit – A simple idea", still seems to apply nearly 50 years after its inception. Design, comfort and quality were the keywords defining ECCO's shoes. In this respect, a direct injection technology – a process in which the upper part of the shoe was placed in a mould before the sole was sprayed directly onto it under extreme pressure – became a cornerstone of ECCO's production. Through this technique, ECCO guaranteed "unrivalled lightness, flexibility and quality in the individual shoe".[26]

In 2008, ECCO encompassed a global organization with 16,300 employees in 33 countries, and it sold 17.5 million pairs of shoes. The company's net revenue was DKK 5.4 billion, while profit was DKK 5.3 million (see Exhibit 1). The organization consisted of 11 business units, in which there were five sales regions, five production units and one leather unit (see Exhibit 2). Each of these units had its own supervisory board, management, budget and financial statements. Headquarters, however, was in charge of the ECCO brand, concept and product development and it also handled central functions, such as logistics, IT and legal services. Karl Toosbuy's daughter, Hanni Toosbuy Kasprzak, was the sole owner of the group. Her husband, Dieter Kasprzak, was the group's CEO.

Products and markets

ECCO produced and sold footwear for all segments under its newly introduced global brand platform – "The most comfortable place on earth" – including business, casual and outdoor shoes for men and women, shoes for children in all ages, and sporting shoes in categories such as golf and leisure. The 2008 sales composition was: ladies, 38.1%; men, 27.2%; kids, 15.2%; and sports, 19.5%. Footwear accounted for 93.8% of total sales, while accessories and leather/wet-blue (chrome-tanned leather) made up the rest (see Exhibit 3). The new brand strategy replaced the "Shoes designed to move you" strategy. One goal was to add an additional comfort dimension to the shoes: "It is a very interesting tension, a comfort/style paradox, we try to pursue…", said Claus Kjærgaard, ECCO's Global Marketing Director, "…partly through the collection, which is moving along a younger and more dynamic course, and through our marketing and communication". The new strategy could also be seen as an attempt to revitalize the perception of ECCO shoes, particularly in Western Europe: "The challenge is the existing perception of the ECCO product as being comfort in an old-fashioned, dusty way," Kjærgaard argued. "We are not repositioning ECCO, but rather peoples' views on comfort".[27]

This tension between the ECCO brand's comfort and fashion aspects was traceable in the development of ECCO's market shares. While Central Europe, Western Europe and North America accounted for 83% of ECCO's total sales in 2004, these regions' significance had fallen to 68% in 2008. In Eastern Europe, on the other hand, ECCO had been nominated as one of the hottest brands in footwear. Accordingly, the company had experienced steep growth – 221% from 2004 to 2008 – and the market had become (together with the Middle East) the group's second largest with DKK 1,143 million in revenue. The Asia/Pacific market had also grown significantly – a 246% increase from 2004 to 2008, with revenue landing at DKK 606 million in 2008 – and now represented 7.7% of total sales. In fact, the Asian market was emphasized by the ECCO group: "Asia was the fastest growing region in ECCO if you look at the last year [2007] and turnover increased by 41%," said Michael Hauge Sørensen, Managing Director of ECCO Asia/Pacific. "We want to do more of the same. Our aim is to double the turnover over the next three years in Asia".[28]

ECCO's global value chain – "From Cow to Customer"

Central to ECCO's corporate strategy was its "from cow to customer'" philosophy, under which the entire process – from the development of an idea, product design, production of leather and shoes to marketing, distribution and wholesale operations – was fully controlled by the company. The internalization of the entire value chain was atypical in the footwear industry, as most of ECCO's competitors, including Geox, Clarks and Timberland, outsourced various aspects (particularly the production phases) to subcontractors in low-cost countries. However, ECCO's management believed that keeping the process in-house was vital to ensuring the quality and standard of shoe production and, consequently, the final product: "We cannot get the best quality if we don't do it ourselves"[29], founder Karl Toosbuy stated. The main drivers behind the company's international outspread had been creation of a market presence, lower labor cost and increased flexibility. Spreading the risk was another important impetus. In fact, ECCO was one of the first Danish companies to offshore its value chain with the establishment of uppers production in Brazil 1974. Yet, although ECCO's activities were spread around the world, they were still kept internal.

ECCO's value chain could be broadly grouped into raw materials, tanning, manufacturing, distribution and wholesale (see Exhibit 4). By 2008, the company owned a global network of tanneries, located in the Netherlands, Thailand, Indonesia and China, which transformed raw hides into various kinds of high-quality leather for ECCO's factories around the world. "Today, we can trace our leather back to an individual cow," explained Parnos Mytaros, Director of ECCO's leather division. "Every shoe has a specific number that shows where and when it is produced, and from which rawhide the leather originated. We need to control the whole chain, or we cannot ensure that the cow has been raised properly, been transported under the right conditions and slaughtered correctly"[30] (see Exhibit 5).

ECCO's leather division was headquartered in Holland, where ECCO, in addition to establishing wet-blue for ECCO's factories, invested extensively in research aimed at achieving more environmentally-friendly production methods. Judging by the scale of ECCO's tanning activities, this research was an important matter. In 2008, ECCO produced 27.8 million square feet of leather and 45.1 million square feet of wet-blue globally. ECCO was therefore among the five largest leather producers in the world, even though this production only accounted for less than 7% of total sales. In aggregate, ECCO controlled 70% of its raw materials, which included raw cattle hides, goat skins and sheep skins. The company also supplied leather to the auto and furniture industries. The bulk of the rawhides came from Germany, France, Denmark and Finland, but it was ECCO's intention to source more input locally to reduce transportation factors. Procurement of raw material took approximately eight weeks from order placement, at which time the materials would be ready to be shipped to the production sites.

In addition to the tanneries, ECCO had a global network of production plants. Its sites in Indonesia, Thailand, Slovakia and China undertook full-scale production of uppers and finished shoes. A plant in Portugal made sales samples and prototypes (this was originally a full-scale production site, but it was scaled down in 2005), and a unit in Denmark was solely responsible for the development and preparation of new articles and prototype testing.

The process of producing ECCO shoes had multiple steps. In the first phase, which was a simple, highly standardized phase, the uppers were cut by hydraulic presses, called clicking machines, before they were attached to the insoles with glue, tacks and staples. These were then placed in an injection-molding machine, where the bottoms of the shoes, including the outsoles and heels, were attached to the uppers under high pressure. This required more sophisticated technology and was the most advanced part of the process. Lastly, each pair of shoes underwent a finishing process, in which the durability and appearance of the shoes were improved through such activities as securing the bottom and trimming the edge (see Exhibit 6). This process suggests that those ECCO's production sites that had a higher relative output of finished shoes (Thailand and Slovakia) were more advanced than the sites that chiefly produced uppers (Indonesia and China). Overall, ECCO produced the vast majority of uppers and shoes in-house. The remainder, which was outsourced, was for shoes that did not benefit from the company's "direct injection" technology. Furthermore, ECCO's production could be divided into five phases: full-scale, benchmarking, ramp-up, prototype and laboratory production.

The objectives of full-scale production were to maintain demand, quality and operational reliability. In 2008, the four full-scale production sites produced a total of 12.6 million pairs of shoes (see Exhibit 7). The benchmarking activities aimed to find areas in which ECCO's different plants could share best practices, and gain knowledge and competencies regarding production cost structures and operational improvements across the board. The ramp-up process investigated how new production systems, based on new products, prototypes and laboratory production technologies coming from ECCO's research and development, could be implemented. The division between the different production sites was not straightforward. Research and development was conducted in Denmark but all of the full-scale production units produced both finished shoes and uppers (with the exception of Slovakia, which only produced finished shoes).

The company had two main distribution centers located in the US and in Tønder, Denmark. The majority of ECCO's shoes went through the center in Tønder, which was expanded in 2001 with the addition of another four warehouses, raising the capacity to two million pairs of shoes. Shoes were distributed to other continents by sea, which took an average of five weeks. However, given the growing importance of the Asian markets, shoes were increasingly shipped directly to the local outlets from the Asian production plants. In addition to the distribution centers, ECCO had five sales units manifesting its global scope: Europe West, Europe Central, Europe East, and Middle East and Asia/Pacific. The shoes were sold in shops entirely dedicated to ECCO, shop-in-shops and factory outlets. In 2008, the number of ECCO stores around the world was 822 (own and partner stores), but the aim was to increase this figure to 1,500 by 2013. 25% of ECCO's retail points were mono-brand stores.

The strategy of internalizing the entire value chain was capital intensive. This could, for instance, be seen in the vast inventory of rawhides and wet-blue, which tied up a great deal of capital. On the other hand, the "from cow to customer" strategy allowed ECCO to maximize productivity and to remain in full control of the quality of production. Production could be carried out more predictably and the company was not as prone to external influences, such as sourcing fluctuations and market irregularities. The risk of ethical misbehavior along the value chain, a problem that companies like Nike had experienced, was reduced. In this respect, ECCO could more easily oblige and control the fulfillment of its Code of Conduct with regards to all value-chain activities (see Exhibit 8). ECCO placed much emphasis on this aspect – as Karl Toosbuy expressed it, "ECCO is a guest in each of the countries in which it operates and shall as such respect the culture of the country".[31] Therefore, although the internalized value chain tied up a substantial amount of money and increased the financial risk, ECCO valued the autonomy and control, which reduced uncertainty and allowed for quality control.

ECCO A/S in China
By the end of 2008, ECCO Xiamen encompassed a production site consisting of five full-scale production plants and one modern tannery. The production plants had been constructed over a period of three years and the tannery was finished in September 2008. Under the management of Morten Bay Jensen, the Chinese production subsidiary had increased the production of uppers from 430,000 in 2005 to 4.1 million in 2008, and the production of shoes had almost doubled over the same period to 900,000 pairs (see Exhibit 9). The DKK 173 million tannery, the largest investment in ECCO's history, was strategically situated close to the production plants. In addition to supplementing ECCO's total leather production, the new tannery was a state-of-the-art facility for sustainable leather production: "ECCO has contributed to raising the standards for leather and shoe production in Xiamen," the city's Vice Major said when the facilities were opened. "We are happy to have the world's most advanced tannery".[32] The tannery consisted of three buildings: the production building, the wastewater treatment unit, and the utilities and warehouse building. According to Mike Redwood, a marketing consultant for the leather industry, the tannery in Xiamen combined new and old production techniques to ensure optimal utilization: "In some areas the

machines are linked in a continuous way using alternate transport, minimizing human intervention". He further explained that "while the machines are new and top quality, the technology being linked together is conventional, as required in a situation where all the companies' plants are making identical leathers. ECCO is a family business and one that understands the scale and scope that needs to come with globalization. They are a second generation Danish footwear company showing the tanning world what is truly possible in our industry".[33]

ECCO's plans to establish production facilities in China dated back to 1993. Even at that time, Karl Toosbuy was eager to begin producing shoes in China. However, after investigating the possibilities, he came to the conclusion that the country was not yet ready for such production and he decided to build a plant in Thailand instead. Twelve years later, ECCO celebrated the opening of the first of five closely connected production plants in Xiamen. These were intended to have a total production capacity of one million pairs of shoes per year by 2008, and they were to serve export needs and the growing Chinese market. "China is one of the most important growth markets in the world", Dieter Kasprzak stated, "and that is one of the reasons that it is important for ECCO to have its own production facilities in this great land".[34]

The choice of Xiamen as ECCO's Chinese production destination was not coincidental. In 2002, Toosbuy himself chaired the group that would decide where ECCO should build its factories in China. After assessing over 40 different locations, he concluded that Xiamen was the most appropriate site. This was mostly a result of the disadvantages associated with other locations. For instance, Toosbuy thought that people were too "moody" in Beijing, and he rejected the many industry parks found across the country because they were, in his eyes, immoral and debasing, as the companies there employed young women who lived living in large sleeping halls. In Xiamen, on the other hand, ECCO could build a factory and still employ local people. "We would rather have people from the local community, and we do not use sleeping halls for our employees", Morten Bay Jensen, ECCO's Managing Director in Xiamen, said. "It is important for us that the employees have a life after work and that they can go home to their families".[35] At the same time, the location in Xiamen was remote enough to avoid the possibility that employees would leave ECCO to work for competitors.

Another impetus for selecting Xiamen as a production site was its status as a special economic zone, which allowed for more liberal economic policies than would be possible in the rest of the country. Companies that allocated their activities to this city were given tax breaks. However, although this created incentives for MNCs considering investments in Xiamen, its significance was downplayed by ECCO: "You can get a few tax benefits from the local authorities…", Karsten Borch, ECCO's Vice Chairman, explained. Borch, who had been highly involved in the establishment of ECCO's Chinese presence, continued"…but only a few.

Strategies in emerging markets

They have a standard clause, called the Most Favored Clause, which states that when the authorities have set a price, others cannot get it cheaper. So there is not much to go after". He also highlighted ECCO's philosophy: "In China, you must earn your money on the basis of a sufficiently effective organization, not through negotiations over tax benefits".[36]

The investments were carried out in cooperation with the Danish Industrial Fund for Developing Countries (IFU). ECCO owned 80% of its assets in China with a share capital of USD 15.6 million, while IFU owned the remaining 20%. The motive for engaging the IFU in this process was not primarily financial: "I'm not looking for IFU's money", Michael Thinghuus, ECCO's Chief Operating Officer explained in 2005. "I could access cheaper money elsewhere. Among other things, we are using IFU to help us through negotiations on the government level".[37]

Dealing with the authorities to gain construction permission had been a highly important, but challenging, task. This aspect was particularly problematic in the footwear industry. The Chinese government had closed numerous tanneries due to poor environmental standards. When ECCO presented its plans for the new tannery in Xiamen, the authorities were accordingly skeptical, as they were opposed, in principal, to the building of polluting facilities. However, ECCO succeeded in convincing the Chinese authorities of its environmental focus in the production phases, and the company received permission shortly thereafter. When he inquired about why the approval process went so quickly, Karsten Borch received the following answer from a secretary of the Communist Party of China: "Our reports indicate that we have not seen anyone with such an advanced treatment system, and it is in our interest that we get this into China. We can then compel other firms to the same high standards".[38] As CEO Dieter Kasprzak expressed it: "The Chinese have come a long way with their environmental laws. We are the last ones that have been allowed to build a tannery in the area".[39]

Dealing with the Dragon
China and Xiamen clearly offered significant potential for ECCO in its pursuit of cost-structure optimization and the production of high-quality footwear. However, producing shoes in China also posed a number of challenges.

One escalating issue was relative cost of producing shoes. Throughout its history, ECCO had been active in offshoring its production to countries with lower salaries, which eventually brought it to China in 2005. In a vastly competitive, global industry, such as the footwear industry, cost optimization was a highly delicate issue for many companies, and China had been a favored choice for many. In Xiamen, ECCO paid its workers an average annual salary of approximately DKK 13,000 and the work week averaged 48 hours. In addition,

ECCO paid roughly DKK 5,500 in employee benefits, such as social security, health insurance, free lunches, social gatherings and a small library. This salary was twice the Chinese minimum (calculated for a 40 hour work week), but was still below the average salary for Xiamen residents of DKK 16,500. "We don't pay the highest salaries", said Morten Bay Jensen, "but they are competitive. It is important for us that the employees have a decent environment, and that we, in return, get what we expect in terms of productivity and efficiency".[40]

However, in recent years, companies had increasingly moved their production processes to countries such as Vietnam and Cambodia, where shoes could be produced by highly qualified personnel at an even lower cost. This trend was another issue that could eventually have an effect on ECCO's competitive position. However, for Dieter Kasprzak, this was not the right strategy to pursue: "We are not moving the production to countries just because they are cheaper", and he argued that "people talk a lot about the fact that salaries and costs are increasing rapidly in China, but it is still cheaper than producing in Europe. And then there is the question of quality".[41] With over half of the world's shoe production taking place in China, production knowledge was sophisticated and the workforce was educated. "We would get poorer quality in Cambodia and Vietnam, and the infrastructure is not good enough", the CEO stated. "For us, it is quality before price".[42]

Another challenge had presented itself in the form of bilateral trade barriers between China and the European Union. In April 2006, only one year after ECCO had commenced Chinese production, the EU placed a 20% tariff on shoes imported from China. The European Commission imposed this tariff after concluding that Chinese shoe manufacturers were receiving "disguised subsidies" from the government and were, consequently, exporting shoes at rates below cost. For ECCO, which was in the process of building its five production plants, this policy had major consequences. First, the company decided to completely halt further expansion of the production facilities. "It is very unfortunate for us that we have already invested so much money in China," commented Michael Thinghuus, "and that we have an infrastructure which might bear considerably more than we are going to produce here".[43] Although, ECCO eventually resumed construction of the production facilities, it sent a larger proportion of semi-finished products from China to countries such as Indonesia and Thailand, where production was completed before the products were shipped to the European markets. In this way, ECCO avoided the trade barriers but incurred higher costs. Lastly, the ongoing "tariff war" between China and the EU left ECCO's management in a situation where uncertainty prevailed. After all, the Chinese government could eventually choose to impose barriers on foreign companies operating in the country.

Although not directly linked to the production of shoes, piracy was also an ongoing challenge to operations in China. A growing number of Chinese shoe producers were plagiarizing and exploiting ECCO's brand and production techniques. "We run into copy products, as do many other Danish companies", Michael Hauge Sørensen, ECCO's Director of Asia/Pacific, said. "Our legal department in Denmark is working with this problem all the time".[44] The ECCO brand was particularly popular in China, and the group repeatedly found cheap copies that abused the ECCO logo. The company was aware that the risks of spin-offs and the leaking of production techniques increased with production located in Xiamen. Low-price generic shoes that suspiciously resembled ECCO's shoes were common on the Chinese market. However, given the company's internalized value-chain approach, ECCO's management felt that it had taken the necessary precautions, particularly with regard to preserving and keeping the production techniques in-house.

* * *

When the chilly rain eventually stopped, Morten Bay Jensen could finally return to streets of Xiamen. He had always enjoyed the clean smell of the air after the rain. However, his mind was too occupied with other things to find pleasure in this now. Well aware of the classical business mantra "think globally – act locally", he could immediately identify two opposing goals. On the one hand, he needed to continue optimizing the local production in Xiamen. This would require development of a business model in which costs were kept as low as possible, while ensuring that product quality was not compromised. He was well aware of the fact that achieving lower production costs had been the initial reason for ECCO's investments in Xiamen. However, the search for lower costs could not be allowed to compromise the production of high-quality shoes.

On the other hand, Bay Jensen had a global responsibility in terms of the ECCO group. With 33% of ECCO's total production of uppers and 7% of its shoe production, as well as ECCO's most expensive investment in the form of the new tannery, the Xiamen facilities constituted a central part of ECCO's global value chain. The issue of ensuring coherent, conducive interfaces between the different value-chain activities and localities was, therefore, an important one. With the decreasing growth in both revenue and profits, Bay Jensen knew that something had to be done in the near future – a great weight was therefore resting on his shoulders.

Exhibits for ECCO A/S case

Exhibit 1 – ECCO's key figures[45]

DKK million	2008	2007	2006	2005	
Income statement					
Net revenue	5,374	5,220	4,470	3,831	3,394
Profit before amortization and depreciation	1,033	1,042	938	629	448
Amortization and depreciation	-206	-209	-178	-205	-181
Profit before financials	827	833	759	424	267
Net financials	-81	-77	-50	-74	-61
Profit before tax	746	756	709	350	206
Income taxes	-172	-193	-209	-125	-43
Profit for the year	527	538	489	226	151
Balance Sheet					
Fixed assets	1,502	1,218	1,121	1,075	1,113
Current assets	2,895	2,997	2,529	2,210	1,833
Assets total	4,397	4,215	3,651	3,285	2,945
Equity	2,473	2,073	1,729	1,286	1,034
Other liabilities	103	73	57	87	57
Debt	1,821	2,069	1,864	1,912	1,854
Liabilities total	4,397	4,215	2,529	2,210	1,833
Cash flow statement					
Cash flow from operating activities	789	264	427	515	273
Cash flow from investing activities	-483	-305	-235	-202	-213
Cash flow from financing activities	-323	-114	-189	-2.4	-0.4
Pairs of shoes sold (`000)	17,559	16,916	14,776	12,906	12,054
Number of employees at the end of the year	16,328	14,957	12,670	10,534	9,657
Key ratios					
Operating margin (%)	15.4	16.0	17.0	11.1	7.9
ROAIC (%)	19.2	21.2	21.9	13.6	9.3
Return on assets (%)	17.3	19.2	20.5	11.2	7.2
Investment ratio	2.3	1.5	1.3	1.0	1.2
Return on equity (%)	23.2	28.3	32.5	19.5	15.2
Solvency ratio (%)	56.3	49.2	47.4	39.1	35.1
Liquidity ratio	1.9	2.2	3.0	2.9	2.0

Strategies in emerging markets

Exhibit 2 – ECCO's organization[46]

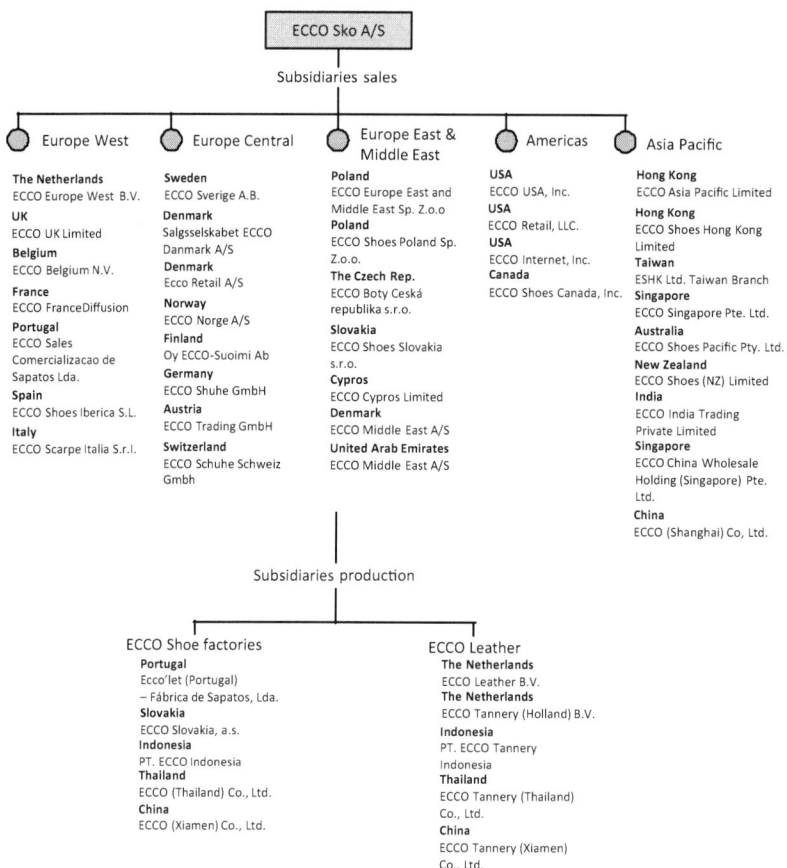

Exhibit 3 – Composition of sales[47]

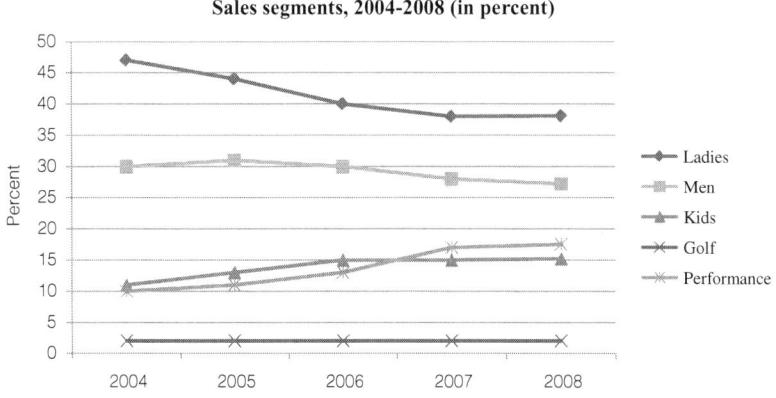

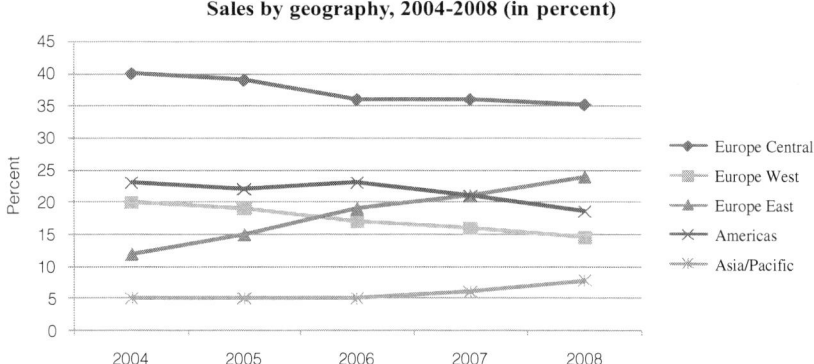

Strategies in emerging markets

Exhibit 4 – ECCO's global value chain[48]

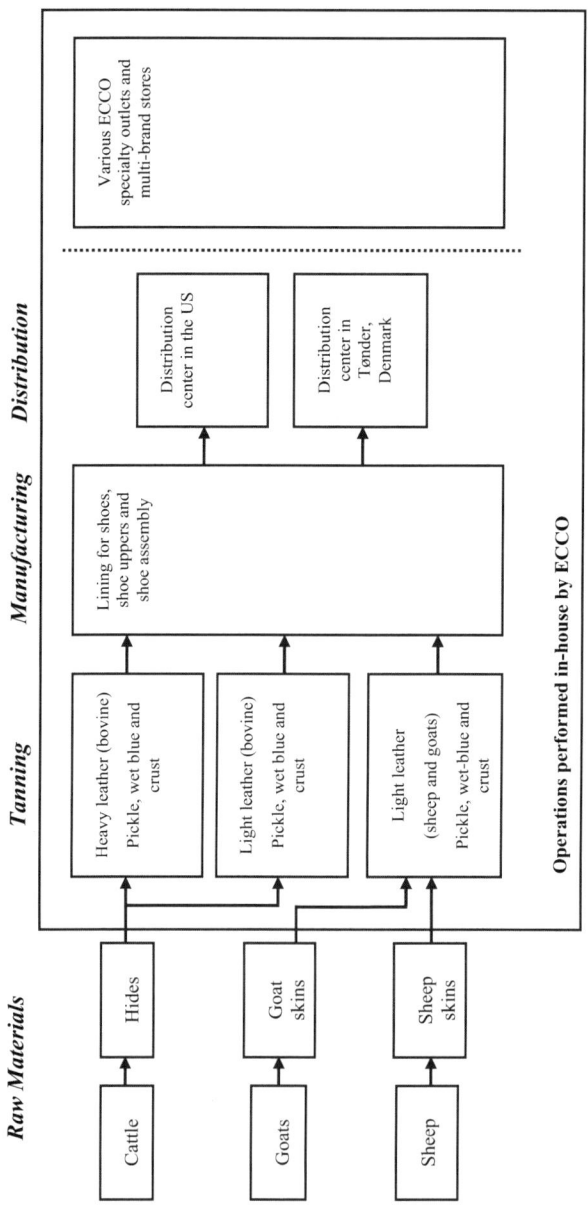

Ecco A/S

Exhibit 5 – Converting skin and hides into leather[49]

Steps in leather production
The production of leather from hides and skins involves the treatment of raw materials, i.e., the conversion of the raw hide or skin, a putrecible material, into leather, a stable material. This material is obtained after passing through the different treatment and processing steps described in points 1 to 4. The production processes in a tannery can be divided into four main categories, though the processes employed in each of these categories may change, depending on the raw material used and the final goods that are to be produced.

1. Hides and skins storage and beam-house operations
Upon delivery, hides and skins can be sorted, trimmed, cured (when the raw material cannot be processed immediately) and stored pending operations in the beam house. The following processes are typically carried out in the beam house of a tannery: soaking, de-haring, liming, fleshing (mechanical scraping off of the excessive organic material) and splitting (mechanically splitting regulates the thickness of hides and skins, splitting them horizontally into a grain layer, and, if the hide is thick enough, a flesh layer).

2. Tannery Operations
Typically the following processes are carried out in the tannery: de-liming, bating, pickling and tanning. Once pickling has been carried out to reduce the pH of the pelt prior to tanning, pickled pelts, i.e., sheepskins can be traded. In the tanning process the collagen fibre is stabilized by the tanning agents so that the hide (the raw material) is no longer susceptible to putrefaction. The two main categories of tanning agents are minerals (trivalent chromium salts) and vegetable (quebracho and mimosa). The tanned hides and skins, once they have been converted to a non-putrescible material called leather, are tradable as intermediate products (wet blue). However, if leather is to be used to manufacture consumer products, it needs further processing and finishing.

3. Post-Tanning Operations
Post-tanning operations generally involve washing out the acids that are still present in the leather following the tanning process. According to the desired leather type to be produced the leather is retanned (to improve the feel and handle of leathers), dyed with water-soluble dyestuffs (to produce even colours over the whole surface of each hide and skin), fat liquored (leathers must be lubricated to achieve product-specific characteristics and to re-establish the fat content lost in the previous procedures) and finally dried. After drying, the leather may be referred to as crust, which is a tradable

intermediate product. Operations carried out in the beam house, the tannery, and the post-tanning areas are often referred to as wet processing, as they are performed in processing vessels filled with water to which the necessary chemicals are added to produce the desired reaction. After post-tanning the leather is dried and subsequent operations are referred to as dry processing. Typically, hides and skins are traded in the salted state, or, increasingly, as intermediate products, particularly in the wet-blue condition for bovine hides and the pickled condition for ovine skins.

4. Finishing Operations

The art of finishing is to give the leather as thin a finish as possible without harming the known characteristics of leather, such as its look and its ability to breathe. The aim of this process is to treat the upper (grain) surface to give it the desired final look. By grounding (applying a base coat to leather to block pores before applying the true finish coats), coating, seasoning, embossing (to create a raised design upon a leather surface by pressure from a heated engraved plate or roller) and ironing (to pass a heated iron over the grain surface of the leather to smooth it and/or to give it a glossy appearance) the leather will have, as desired by fashion, a shiny or matt, single or multi-coloured, smooth or clearly grained surface. The overall objective of finishing is to enhance the appearance of the leather and to provide the appropriate performance characteristics in terms of colour, gloss, and handling, among others.

Exhibit 6 – Composition of an ECCO shoe[50]

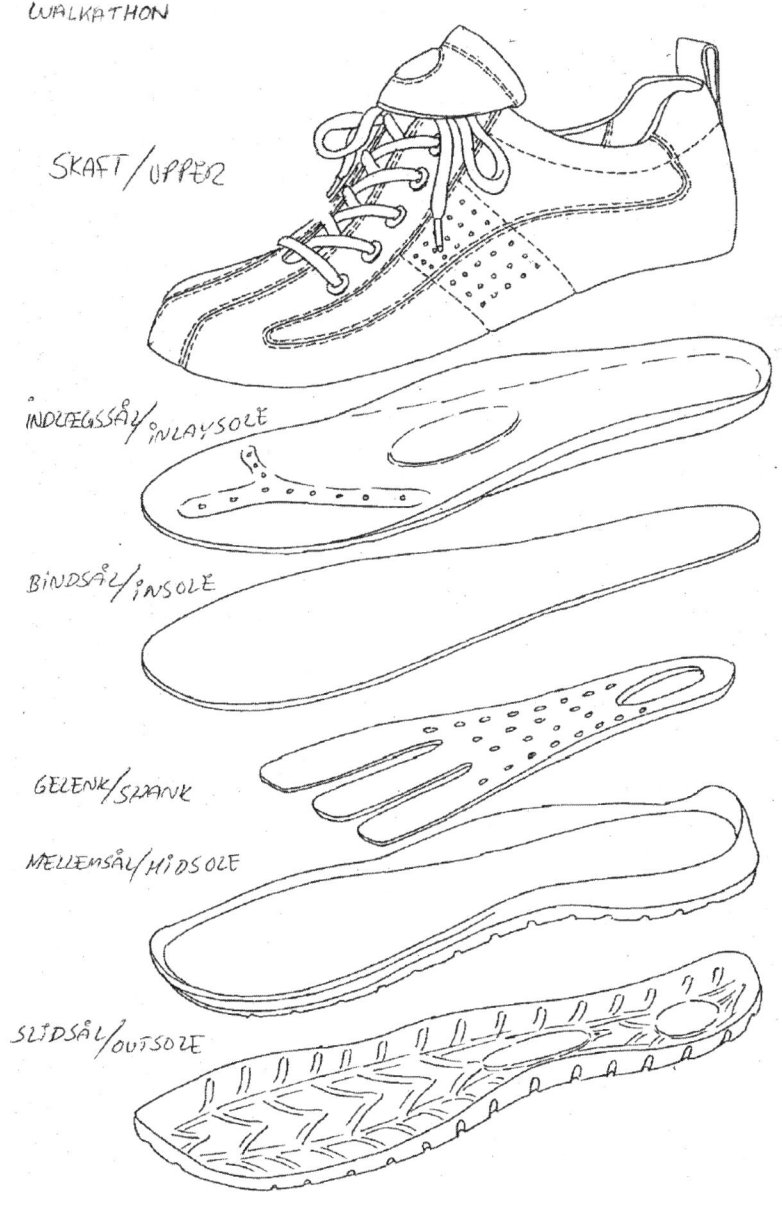

Strategies in emerging markets

Exhibit 7 – ECCO's production output worldwide 2004-2008[51]

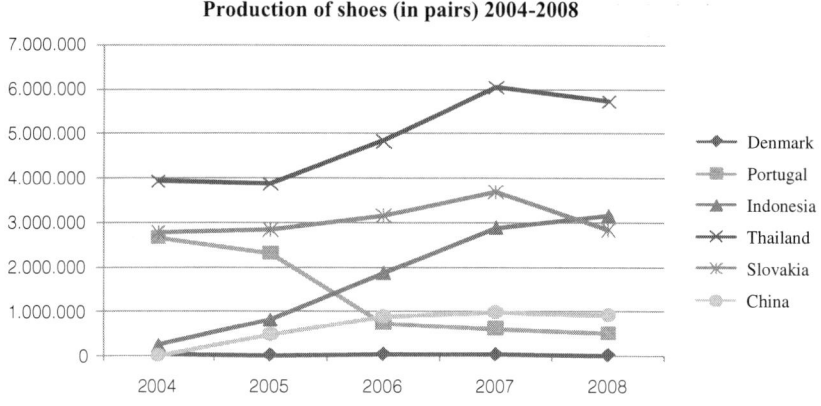

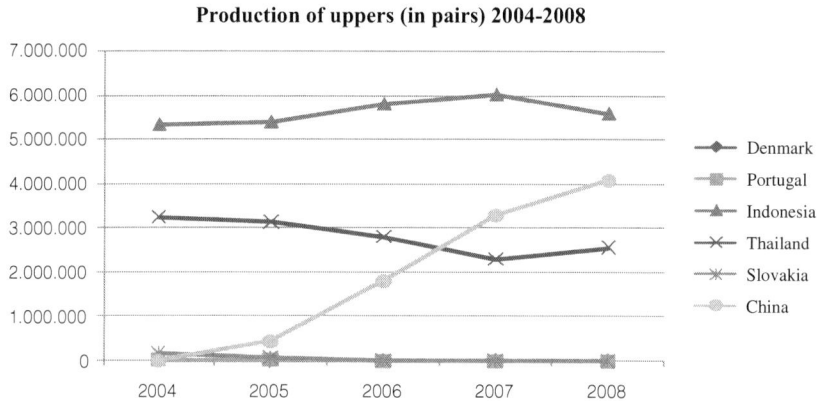

Ecco A/S

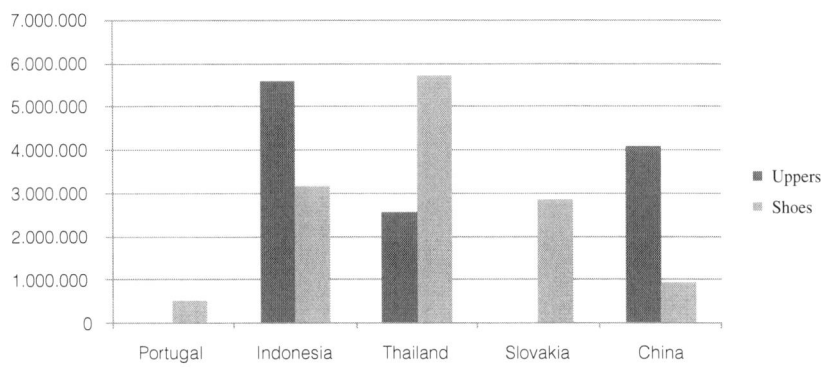

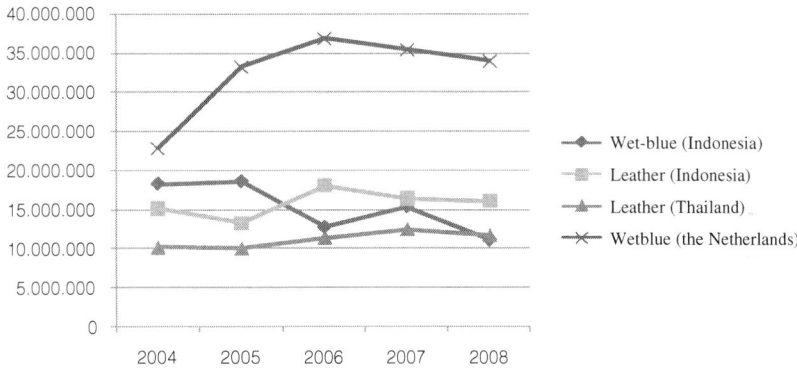

Strategies in emerging markets

Exhibit 8 – The ECCO Code of Conduct[52]

ECCO'S 10 COMMITMENTS

1. ECCO is a guest in each of the countries in which it operates and will as such respect the culture of the individual country.
2. ECCO supports, respects and has a proactive approach to the protection of internationally defined human rights.
3. ECCO respects equal opportunities and supports abolishment of discrimination in the workplace.
4. ECCO respects a person's right to freedom of religion.
5. ECCO respects the right to freedom of association.
6. ECCO wishes employees to have access to a workplace free of harassment or abuse and condemns any forms of compulsory labour.
7. ECCO supports the UN Convention on the Rights of the Child.
8. ECCO provides training, education and further development of human resources on all levels.
9. ECCO aims to be a leading company in the area of environment, health and safety and aims to promote sustainable development.
10. ECCO wishes to ensure that the conduct of its business as an absolute minimum always comply with all relevant laws and regulations.

Exhibit 9 – Key figures from ECCO Xiamen[53]

	2008	2007	2006	2005
Employees	3,210	2,971	2,090	916
Production output				
Uppers produced (pairs)	4,074,456	3,297,987	1,793,505	428,076
Shoes produced (pairs)	908,602	967,517	867,642	475,724
Energy and water consumption				
Electricity (MWh)	6,824	6,052	4,412	3,435
Oil (l)	5,274	10,312	8,415	-
Water (m2)	60,125	47,495	29,882	23,096
Consumption of sole material				
Polyol and icocyanate (kg)	366,030	382,677	322,974	152,479
TPU (kg)	47,800	63,481	97,697	-
Hardener (kg)	18,360	21,342	18,557	7,744
Color paste (kg)	6,609	5,350	5,793	2,945
Release (kg)	2,820	3,777	2,635	1,133
Finishing products (kg)	12,388	18,954	4,793	2,046
Waste				
Recyclable waste (tons)	229	229	193	8.4
Waste otherwise disposed of (tons)	448	464	334	0.5
Chemical waste (tons)	4.2	5.8	3.7	3.6

CHAPTER 4

Casting the global turnaround of FLSmidth – The Indian case

Anders Bech, Managing Director of FLSmidth & Co. A/S's Indian operations, sat in his spacious office, which overlooked the massive office complexes along Old Mahabalipuram Road in the southern part of Chennai. The quietness of the office in this sprawling, dusty southern Indian industrial city was only interrupted by the subtle humming of the air conditioner and occasional noises from the neighboring construction site, where the large Danish producer of equipment and plants for cement and minerals processing was raising a new, four-story office building.

Bech could not help but smile as he thought about the astonishing success story of FLSmidth India. Since his arrival just four years ago in 2004, the Indian subsidiary of FLSmidth had grown from being small, sleepy outpost in a dormant Indian market into the largest FLSmidth site in the world. The subsidiary now possessed a key mandate in the global strategy. By 2008, Bech was in charge of almost 3,000 employees, compared to merely 500 in 2003, which constituted more than 30% of the group's total work force and outnumbered any other single location by far. The Indian subsidiary was not only serving the rapidly growing Indian market, but was also catering to export markets. Moreover, highly skilled engineers had recently been employed to handle increasingly advanced projecting and design functions related to cement and minerals processing. Anders Bech knew that the tremendous success of the Indian subsidiary was not the result of his and his Indian colleagues' ingenuity alone. It was, to a large extent, the result of a conscious and felicitous strategy adopted by FLSmidth's management in the early 2000s, when it found itself in the midst of one of the worst crises in the company's history.

The crises of FLSmidth

FLSmidth & Co. A/S was founded by Frederik Læsøe Smidth in Frederiksberg, Denmark, in 1882 as a one-man engineering consultancy. The company quickly grew into a full-fledged producer of plant and machinery for cement and other

Strategies in emerging markets

construction materials. Over time, it became a global leader in the supply of equipment, complete solutions and after-sales services in the cement industry. In addition, it operated numerous cement production facilities around the world and it was one of the first Danish multinational firms.

In the early 2000s, however, the company faced huge losses and struggled to manage an increasingly diverse portfolio of activities. The company had experienced a massive decline in turnover from DKK 20,993 million in 1999 to DKK 8,939 million in 2003 and it appeared that the "company gold" was vanishing into thin air. Moreover, during the boom years that preceded the millennium shift, the group had diversified into a vast array of industries, such as environmental technology and aerospace. Each of these parts seemed to be pursuing its own, uncoordinated goals.

Therefore, when the new CEO, Jørgen Huno Rasmussen, took the helm of the FLSmidth Group in January 2004, he faced some daunting challenges in terms of restructuring and refocusing the group. In addition to the need to refocus the core business and return to profitability, the company faced intensifying competition and dwindling market shares in its core business, cement production, a business in which low-cost competitors were gaining a foothold, especially in China. Consequently, the ensuing dramatic restructuring of the company encompassed several measures: a restructuring of the company's organizational and ownership structure, a focus on the core businesses of minerals processing, and a strategy aimed at addressing the challenge posed by low-cost competitors. Central to this strategy was the growing, pivotal role of FLSmidth India.

FLSmidth: "One source – one partner"
Organization
From its inception, FLSmidth had been controlled by the holding company Potagua, which was owned by FLSmidth's founding families. Under the leadership of Huno Rasmussen, however, the company became a publicly traded company in 2005. 51% of the shares were sold and only one shareholder – the Danish pension scheme ATP – was reported to control an interest of more than 5%. This was in stark contrast to the earlier setup, where the majority of shares were owned by Potagua. In fact, the organizational and financial turmoil that culminated with significant losses in 2003 and 2004 could, at least in part, be ascribed to the previous ownership structure.

FLSmidth's new group structure consisted of executive group management, headed by Huno Rasmussen, and three company groups: Cements, Minerals, and Cembrit (see Exhibits 2 and 3). Cembrit, which was active in fiber cement products used in construction, had few technological or marketing connections with the core divisions of Cements and Minerals. Cements and Minerals each consisted of a divisional headquarters, a number of geographically oriented project subdivisions, and a number of proprietary equipment companies located mainly in Europe and North America.

In focusing on the integration of the two divisions, FLSmidth's management aimed to harvest the synergies of technology, knowledge and resource overlaps. Organizationally, however, the divisions differed somewhat. In addition to two project divisions at its headquarters in Valby, Denmark, Cements had a project division in Chennai, India and a project division in Bethlehem, Pennsylvania. The Minerals headquarters was located in Bethlehem and served as a full-service office with sales, engineering and project execution services.[54] Moreover, both groups had regional sales offices on all continents. FLSmidth operated two R&D laboratories: one in Mariager, Denmark and another in Chennai, India. R&D was undertaken by the individual product companies.

The company's value chain took several different configurations based on the type of product and services offered. Engineering was mainly an internal resource, while equipment was assembled by the different European and American FLSmidth product companies. The high-tech machines and certain spare parts were produced in-house, while the rest of the production was outsourced. Indeed, 80% to 90% of the manufacturing of machinery was outsourced, corresponding to roughly 65% of the company's costs.[55] However, the company also had its own in-house manufacturing plants, which included a 190,000 square foot plant in Mannheim, Pennsylvania, a spare part foundry in Chennai, India, and a large machine shop in Qingdao, China.

Products and markets

FLSmidth considered itself to be a knowledge firm with strong focus on energy efficiency and environmental responsibility. The company's vision was to continuously strengthen "its position as the preferred partner and leading supplier of equipment and services to the global cement and minerals industries" as well as to continuously "generate a profitable return…".[56] The FLSmidth slogan "One source – One partner" captured its business concept of serving as a one-stop-shop. This meant that it was able to assist customers with the establishment, management, and after-sales aspects of cement and mineral processing plants. FLSmidth's product portfolio consisted of a complete range of products for cement and mineral producers, ranging from entire plants to equipment and services that the customers would need for any point in the production process. It was a "cradle-to-grave" concept. Although the company used to produce cement, it had decided to focus on providing machinery, plants and services that were needed for cement production. After-sales services, such as day-to-day operations and maintenance of production facilities, were becoming increasingly important and accounted for 21% of the consolidated Cements and Minerals turnover in 2007 (see Exhibit 4).

Strategies in emerging markets

Although it was a highly diversified conglomerate at the turn of the millennium, FLSmidth became a business that provided plants, machinery and services for two core markets: the cement and minerals markets. For each of these markets, the company's product strategies were generally similar: delivery of machinery, processes and plant designs, as well as lifelong customer services, including plant management and maintenance. Traditionally, the cement activities had dominated. However, by 2008, Minerals and Cements were converging in size, representing turnovers of DKK 10.5 billion and DKK 13.7 billion, respectively.

The two-market strategy was justified on the basis of the overlapping basic technologies, knowledge and resources between the two industries. In addition, the presumed counter-cyclical character of the two industries, in which cyclical downturns in one could be offset by opposite fluctuations in the other, supported the two-pronged strategy. Moreover, the continued growth in after-market services was seen as a way to guard against cyclical fluctuations in the two industries. Overall, the projecting and delivery of plants was viewed as the most cyclical, whereas the delivery of specific proprietary products was less cyclical and customer services were only slightly cyclical. Of the three, the latter two constituted approximately 40-50% of the company's turnover, and their share of the product mix was expected to increase (see Exhibit 5).

The company possessed a wide range of proprietary equipment, including Maag Gear, Ventomatic packing machines, different brands of roller and separator mills (OK, Excel, SAG, etc.), Krebs hydrocyclone classification equipment, and the gigantic ore conecrushers used in mining. Other examples of products included handling and transportation equipment, such as conveyor belts, elevators and slides.

Financial performance

By 2008, FLSmidth had experienced a considerable financial improvement from previous years (see Exhibit 1). The 2008 Annual Report showed that the group – with an equity ratio of 24% – had a return on shareholder equity of 33% and a profit margin of 9.5%. These figures can be compared to the lows of a -59% return on shareholder equity in 2003 and a profit margin of -1.8% in 2004. The 2008 profit margin for Cement was 11.9%, while it was 12.5% for Minerals. This should be seen in relation to the total assets of each division of DKK 13.7 billion and DK 13.0 billion, respectively. In addition, FLSmidth operated with a relatively low – at times, even negative – working capital due to fluctuations in customer prepayments.[57]

Competitive strategy

FLSmidth had a global market share in the cement industry (excluding the

Chinese market) of about one-third in 2007 (compared to 50-60% in 2003). The company was experiencing increasing competitive pressure from low-cost emerging market competitors, such as China's Sinoma, which held 24% of the global market. Sinoma was a provider of machinery and services, covered the same business segments as FLSmidth Cements and was the largest player in China. While Sinoma was the overall global market leader in terms of global market share (including China), FLSmidth remained largest in terms of the size of deliverable cement production plants. Other major global competitors were Polysius (19% market share) and KHD (12%; see Exhibit 6).

In order to maintain its leading global market position, FLSmidth strived to constantly be at the technological frontier of its industries. Its ambition was to at least introduce one main machinery, process invention or improvement every year. Indeed, FLSmidth claimed to be a technological leader in the market and it viewed technology as a central parameter in the face of Chinese competition, which was based on lower costs. Consequently, R&D was given high priority. Continually high levels of development and design were necessary to maintain a "technological edge on the competition".[58] In 2007, the company spent DKK 210 million, or 1.1% of the total turnover, on R&D. The R&D budget for 2009 was expanded to DKK 350 million.[59]

Competition in the minerals segment was somewhat different from competition in the cement segment, as FLSmidth "only" had two competitors in the same overall business range. One was Batemann Engineering, which covered the same range of product and mineral segments, despite its smaller size. The other was Metso Minerals, which appeared to cover a slightly smaller number of segments, but had net sales of approximately DKK 19.4 billion in 2007, making it larger than FLSmidth Minerals in terms of turnover. In addition to Bateman and Metso, a number of actors operated in smaller, isolated parts of FLSmidth's overall range of segments (see Exhibit 7).

In order to achieve its goal of becoming world leader, FLSmidth's overall group strategy focused on, *inter alia,* reducing costs and increasing efficiency. Therefore, the company was working on "strengthening technological leadership by increasing investments in research and development, optimizing the cost structure by implementing LEAN processes, offshoring engineering work to India and increased sourcing in low-cost countries, and global integration between Cement and Minerals to enhance knowledge sharing and utilization of resources".[60] FLSmidth's presence in India – and India's "presence" in FLSmidth – became a cornerstone of this strategy.

Casting the Indian case

FLSmidth was active on all continents by 2008. Two-thirds of its turnover in 2008 was generated in developing countries (see Exhibit 8). The largest country, by far, in terms of operations in the developing world was India.

Strategies in emerging markets

Earlier, however, FLSmidth's Indian operations had led a relatively secluded life with little growth and difficulties in integrating the Indian operations with FLSmidth's global operations. The company had – under different guises – been present in the country for many years. The first FLSmidth cement factory in India was built in 1902. After India gained its independence in 1947, strong import substitution policies were introduced, which meant that FLSmidth could only continue its Indian activities through licensing. In 1984, however, the situation changed. After entering into a joint venture with the US-based Fuller Company (which it fully acquired in 1990 together with a subsidiary in Chennai, Tamil Nadu), FLSmidth's operations took off in earnest. At the time, the company was also present in India through a licensing agreement with the largest Indian engineering company Larsen & Toubro. Larsen & Toubro was established in the 1930s by two previous FLSmidth employees but it was expropriated shortly after India's independence and turned into a locally owned company by the Indian government.

Therefore, FLSmidth had a long history of activities in India but the operations had been relatively secluded and isolated from group's overall strategy. This changed as FLSmidth shifted management and corporate strategy in 2003-2004. In its new corporate strategy, India was assigned a key role and top management, headed by CEO Huno Rasmussen, devoted dedicated attention to the implementation of the Indian strategy, which spun around two axes: a market strategy and a resource strategy.

As a result of the Indian market strategy and favorable developments in the Indian market, the company experienced remarkable expansion in the following years and overall Asia's contribution to group turnover rose from DKK 2,082 million in 2003 to DKK 7,254 million in 2008.

Recruitment of Indian engineers was a cornerstone of the resource strategy. The sourcing of engineering activities had been underway for quite some time. The former CEO, Birger Riisager, had noted that if FLSmidth wished to expand at some point, then the hiring of engineers would happen not in Denmark but in India or similar low-cost countries.[61] In fact, there was a steady expansion of engineering activities in India prior to 2003-2004. However, it was only after Huno Rasmussen became CEO in 2003 that India began to be viewed as a resource rather than merely a large market. It was now argued that tasks that had traditionally been undertaken by the FLSmidth technology centers in the US and Europe should increasingly be transferred to Chennai. All standard operations were to be concentrated in India, while new staff hired in Denmark would primarily be highly specialized employees, such as those working within R&D. The sourcing of activities was not only motivated by cost reductions but also by a need to deal with the dwindling availability of staff to perform advanced engineering services in Denmark and the US. With its seemingly endless supply of highly skilled engineers, India was the perfect resource base for FLSmidth.

Another strength of the Indian location in terms of resources was its increasingly competent local supply industry. In time, FLSmidth would source basic materials and components from nearly 200 local vendors, to whom the company provided detailed designs.

Apart from market and resource advantages, the Indian location possessed two additional advantages: the widespread use of the English language and the relatively well-functioning legal protection for intellectual property rights (IPR). Given India's British colonial heritage, interaction among the main divisions of FLSmidth posed no barrier on a linguistic level. Moreover, India had much more effective IPR enforcement than some other countries, such as China.

Implementing the Indian strategy

As management was developing its Chennai strategy, it decided to assign the seasoned FLSmidth manager Anders Bech to run the Indian affairs. Management felt it was essential to send an FLSmidth man to India. As noted by N. Shankar, a member of the FLSmidth India Board, an Indian CEO would not be able to overcome the psychological barriers that would obstruct the expansion of the Indian operations and move FLSmidth India toward the next phase of services as a truly global resource.[62]

Although he was unable to hide his Danish traits, Anders Bech was not just another foreigner coming to India. He was, in many ways, a personification of the increasingly global nature of FLSmidth, having worked only a few years of his 20 years with the company in Denmark. Before coming to Chennai in 2004, Bech had been stationed in France, Thailand, Brazil and Italy. Bridging gaps between cultures had, therefore, been an everyday activity throughout his career. Accordingly, in India, he worked at breaking down barriers, and encouraging knowledge sharing and better communication from day one. Indeed, the challenges ahead of him required all of his communicative and organizational skills.

The challenges of moving from routine work to higher value-adding activities

Initially, the engineering work carried out in India was of a more routine character. The main assignments undertaken by the engineers in Chennai were related to product engineering, including the drawing up of plans for the plants. The more complex, knowledge-intensive, higher value-adding tasks were primarily undertaken in Denmark and the US, either in-house by FLSmidth or by the many proprietary product companies. These tasks included designing process and plant layouts, price calculations, procurement, logistics, contract negotiations and on-site management (inspection and troubleshooting). The latter was particular important in terms of ensuring that the plants ran properly after they had been built, and required skills that only an experienced engineer could possess. Another important task, which was mainly carried out in Denmark, was the drafting of work manuals. These manuals were used to make the embodied and tacit knowledge, experience, and routines of the company and its employees, explicit. They were designed to ensure that engineers who were situated in different parts of the world would follow the same standards.

As the Indian engineers in Chennai broadened their experience, knowledge and understanding of the FLSmidth products, however, management was faced with the choice of whether to attempt to transfer higher value-adding R&D activities to India. With quality and technology leadership being two of FLSmidth's main competitive strengths, the question was whether the innovative capacity necessary to stay at the technological frontier could be guaranteed if these tasks were undertaken in Chennai. "As a point of departure, Indians are extremely good at repairing things, but they are not traditionally trained in thinking innovatively,"[63] Anders Bech commented. The Indian tradition of clear divisions and hierarchies, which tended to leave employees with less motivation in their daily work, posed a further challenge in terms of innovation activities. Moreover, Indian employees were known for their tendency to be rather unwilling to share knowledge, as they believed that possession of unique knowledge was important in terms of job security.

Nevertheless, Bech was optimistic, explaining that "we are trying to educate them… by involving everybody as much as possible".[64] In this respect, Bech initiated five steps that were designed to implement a more innovative working culture in Chennai. These were: testing of managers' strengths and weaknesses; building of an organization with five layers; defining career possibilities within the company; result-based pay; and giving increased HR-responsibility to team managers.[65] He hoped that system would help Indian employees become more receptive to knowledge sharing and that it would support their engagement in innovative activities. Ultimately, although he was skeptical of the innovative capacity of Indian culture, Anders Bech did "not see any limits to the type of assignments that can be solved in India. There is no difference in the quality of the work carried out in India or Denmark if one secures the proper training of employees".[66]

The challenges of integrating with the Danish operations
Another challenge faced by the Indian operation was to strike a balance between Danish management and local management. One initiative undertaken at the group level was to invite 20-25 top managers from all parts of the world to participate in an annual joint management program.[67] On the operational level, however, the exchange of knowledge, and the facilitation of dialogues and collaborations among colleagues working in different parts of the world was handled through the implementation of an integrated, global IT platform and the

establishment of an in-house, 24/7 help desk. The former was based in Denmark with the majority of IT personnel situated in India, while the latter was entirely outsourced to India. However, achieving optimal utilization of the global reach of FLSmidth in relation to the composition of nationalities and cultures was far from easy. Countless possibilities of misunderstandings existed, and it was a problem that management would continuously have to consider.

The challenges of recruitment and infrastructure

FLSmidth's management had devised a strategy in which a greater proportion of the company's engineering work was to be done in India as the Indian operation expanded. Eventually, the Indian engineers in Chennai carried out around 70% of the work on all global cement projects.[68] With the growing capacity and assignments came a need for rapidly increasing the number of Indian engineers. Every year in India, 70,000 engineers finished their formal education. However, 9 out of 10 students graduating from the best schools already had an employment contract three months before they finished their last exams. Early on, therefore, FLSmidth management decided to strengthen its human resources in India, where recruitment and retainment became a key priority for management.

56% of FLSmidth's Indian staff was under 30 years old and was rather mobile. The knowledge-intensive work that FLSmidth handled required a certain amount of training and experience. FLSmidth's attrition rate had nearly halved since 2004 to around 10% by 2007 compared to the national average of approximately 20%.[69] Therefore, although there was an increasing demand for highly qualified engineers in India, FLSmidth had generally been successful in recruiting and retaining its staff of engineers. This had been achieved through a number of initiatives. Not only were the employees given pay raises of 25% to 50% annually,[70] results-based pay could further increase their total pay by up to 30%. Moreover, Indian employees were offered attractive career opportunities in terms of in-service training in the US or Denmark. According to Anders Bech, this possibility was very appealing to Indian employees.[71] As Board Member N. Shankar commented: "India is not just another outpost where one can get the cheapest machine production in the world. India can offer a lot of brainpower, which is needed in the west – and that is why it is not about anyone losing anything, but about everyone getting an extra share".[72]

Another major challenge facing Bech was related to Indian infrastructure. FLSmidth India was located in the outskirts of Chennai. Ironically, although FLSmidth could be a key player in supplying India with the raw materials it needed to improve its patchwork infrastructure, the planned highway that was supposed to pass FLSmidth's facilities some 25 kilometers outside the city had yet to be finalized. Half of the highway was laid, while the rest was partly earth and partly asphalt, and filled with potholes, with hectic traffic and Indian cows plodding around in the middle of the road. As Anders Bech pointed out, one of India's biggest problems was that things often were left undone because no one took responsibility.[73] As a result of the deficient infrastructure, FLSmidth had to organize its own transport services to enable employees to get to and from work.

* * *

Anders Bech was pleased with the tremendous success that FLSmidth India had achieved over the past four years. A number of challenges related to the massive expansion had been addressed, if not resolved, and the Indian operation was destined to grow in the years to come. By 2008, with a history of extremely high growth rates, with almost 3,000 employees and with the general support of the other engineering divisions in Denmark and the US, the Chennai offices served as a pivotal strategic and economic basis for the entire FLSmidth Group. However, despite, or maybe because of, its growing strategic significance in the FLSmidth Group, tensions between Denmark and India were rising, posing a new challenge for Anders Bech.

Until that point, the massive expansion of engineering services in India rested on a generally tacit covenant between management and employees that expansion in India would not happen at the expense of employment in Denmark. Therefore, despite the dramatic increase in staff in India, a retrenchment among FLSmidth engineers in Denmark had, by and large, been avoided. Instead, sufficient capacity and cost-competitiveness had simply been secured through the expansion of facilities in India, which was financed by the increasing global and Indian demand. Even though the salaries of Danish engineers in the cement segment were six times higher than those of Indian engineers, retaining Danish engineers had been necessary due to the fact that much of the knowledge related to designing and developing minerals processing systems was tacit and embodied in the Danish workforce. Moreover, the required expertise for the initial building of the Chennai facilities was mainly located in Denmark. Naturally, the increase in the Chennai staff, and the growing importance of their role in drawing up cement and mineral plants had, at times, been met with resistance in Denmark, as this was regarded as a potential threat to Danish jobs.[74] To address these concerns, management communicated a fine distinction between routine tasks and R&D. CEO Huno Rasmussen insisted that FLSmidth only "exports the most routine tasks and assignments" and "collects all our product development activities in Denmark, where we are better placed to protect them against copying".[75]

However, the external conditions for the smooth transition to India had evaporated by late 2008. Amid growing problems related to the global financial crises, FLSmidth announced in 2009 that it would reduce its workforce by roughly 600 employees. The reductions would mainly affect the project centers in Bethlehem and Valby, while Chennai would only be affected to a limited extent. This was the latest manifestation of the group's structural transformation, which had been underway for years, a transformation in which Indian staff became involved in an increasing number of complex, higher value-adding tasks. As India became capable of performing increasingly advanced tasks, the justification for maintaining the higher Danish and US salaries was weakened. Moreover, the vast workforce of highly skilled Indian engineers would not accept performing routine tasks, in the long run, while overall design and development took place in the north. If FLSmidth was to attract and retain the best staff in India, it would need to offer better career and development opportunities for its Indian personnel.

Anders Bech sensed that the Indian operation was moving into a new phase. After a frantic expansion, it was time for consolidation and integration. This phase would not necessarily be easy; further developing the tasks performed in India while maintaining internal coherence in the organization would be a huge challenge that would require his full attention in the coming months. He would have to facilitate the bridging of cultural differences and overcome resistance within the FLS group to the expansion of the mandate of the Indian operation. Glancing out the window of his modern Chennai office, Anders Bech was already contemplating his next move.

Exhibits for FLSmidth A/S case

Exhibit 1 – FLSmidth's key figures [76]

Group financial highlights DKKm	2004	2005 1)	2006 1)	2007	2008	2008 2)
INCOME STATEMENT						
Revenue	10.597	10.250	12.311	19.967	25.285	3.391
Gross profit	1.412	1.908	2.602	4.272	5.621	754
Earnings before non-recurring items, depreciation, amortisation (EBITDA)	142	558	966	2.100	2.911	390
Earnings before interest and tax (EBIT)	-186	398	775	1.824	2.409	323
Earnings before tax (EBT)	-196	512	924	1.877	2.123	285
Profit/loss for the year, continuing activities	-330	530	1.107	1.293	1.456	195
Profit/loss for the year, discontinuing activities	481	-54	25	1	59	8
Profit/loss for the year	151	476	1.132	1.294	1.515	203
CASH FLOW						
Cash flow from operating activities	-299	1.731	1.288	1.493	2.324	312
Acquisition of enterprises and activities	-3	-47	-190	-3.409	-210	-28
Acquisition of tangible assets	-148	-176	-249	-386	-627	-84
Other investments, net	26	279	52	-18	-34	-5
Cash flow from investing activities	-125	56	-387	-3.813	-871	-117
Cash flow from operating and investing activities of continuing activities	-424	1.787	976	-2.448	1.492	200
Cash flow from operating and investing activities of discontinuing activities	4.122	21	-75	128	-39	-5
WORKING CAPITAL	878	-240	-435	665	207	28
NET INTEREST-BEARING RECEIVABLES/(DEBT)	1.191	2.600	2.847	-1.583	-574	-77
ORDER INTAKE (GROSS)	8.459	13.289	18.534	24.131	30.179	4.050

| ORDER BACKLOG | 6.506 | 10.834 | 18.264 | 25.361 | 30.485 | 4.092 |

BALANCE SHEET						
Non-current assets	1.745	1.913	2.355	7.799	8.255	1.108
Current assets	6.448	7.664	9.764	11.865	12.474	1.674
Assets held for sale	0	0	132	8	8	1
Total assets	8.193	9.577	12.251	19.672	20.737	2.783
Consolidated equity	2.585	2.648	3.192	4.214	5.035	676
Long-term liabilities	1.130	1.271	1.710	4.826	4.103	550
Short-term liabilities	4.478	5.658	7.344	10.632	11.599	1.557
Liabilities regarding assets held for sale	0	0	5	0	0	0
Total equity and liabilities	8.193	9.577	12.251	19.672	20.737	2.783

| PROPOSED DIVIDEND TO SHAREHOLDERS | 372 | 372 | 372 | 372 | 0 | 0 |

FINANCIAL RATIOS						
Continuing activities						
Contribution ratio	13,3%	18,6%	21,1%	21,4%	22,2%	22,2%
EBITDA ratio	1,3%	5,4%	7,8%	10,5%	11,5%	11,5%
EBIT ratio	-1,8%	3,9%	6,3%	9,1%	9,5%	9,5%
EBIT ratio before effect of purchase price allocations regarding GL&V Process	-1,8%	3,9%	6,3%	9,9%	10,6%	10,6%
EBT ratio	-1,9%	5,0%	7,5%	9,4%	8,4%	8,4%
Return on equity	5,5%	18,2%	38,8%	34,9%	32,8%	32,8%
Equity ratio	31,6%	27,6%	26,1%	21,4%	24,3%	24,3%
Number of employees at 31 December, Group	5.625	5.849	6.862	9.377	11.510	11.510

FLSmidth

Number of employees in Denmark	1.642	1.463	1.508	1.657	1.871	1.871
Share and dividend ratios, Group						
CFPS (cash flow per share), (diluted)	-5,7	33,0	24,5	28,4	44,2	5,9
EPS (earnings per share), (diluted)	2,8	9,1	21,6	24,6	28,8	3,9
EPS (earnings per share), (diluted) before the effect of purchase price allocations						
regarding GL&V Process	-	-	-	26	33	4
Net assets value per share, (parent company)	50	46	38	46	49	7
Dividend per share	7	7	7	7	0	0
Pay-out ratio (%)	243,0%	77,0%	32,0%	29,0%	0,0%	0,0%
FLSmidth & Co. share price	102,4	186	359	522	181	24
Number of shares, 31 December (000s)	53.200	53.200	53.200	53.200	53.200	53.200
Average number of shares (000s) (diluted)	52.509	52.518	52.558	52.640	52.544	52.544
Market capitalisation	5.448	9.895	19.099	27.770	9.629	1.292

The financial ratios have been computed in accordance with the Guidelines issued by the Danish Society of Financial Analysts.

1) The financial highlights for 2005 to 2006 are prepared in accordance with the change in accounting policy in 2006 in respect of measurement of financial assets pursuant to the changed IAS 39. In accordance with the transition, provisions for the changed IAS 39 implementation has therefore taken place retroactively from 1 January 2005.

2) Income statement items are translated at the average EUR exchange rate of 745.55, and the balance sheet and cash flow items are translated at the year-end EUR exchange rate of 745.06.

Exhibit 2 – Group structure[77]

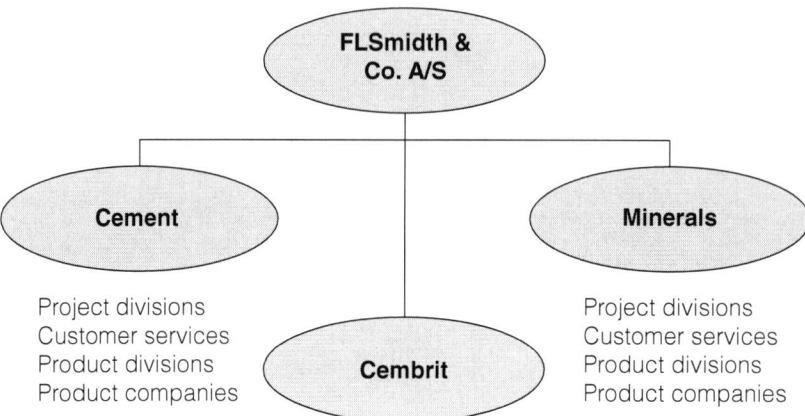

Exhibit 3 – Organization[78]

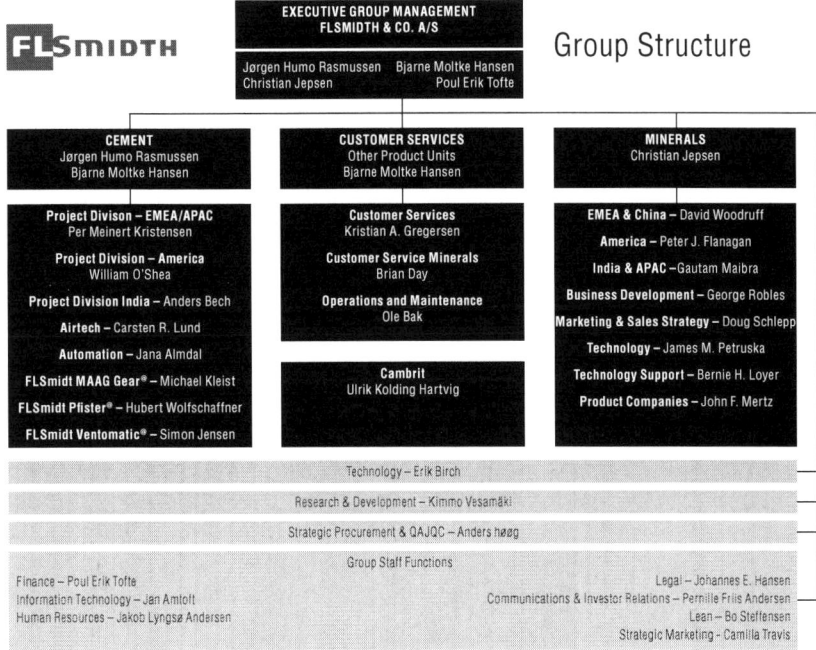

Strategies in emerging markets

Exhibit 4 – Cement and minerals production process[79]

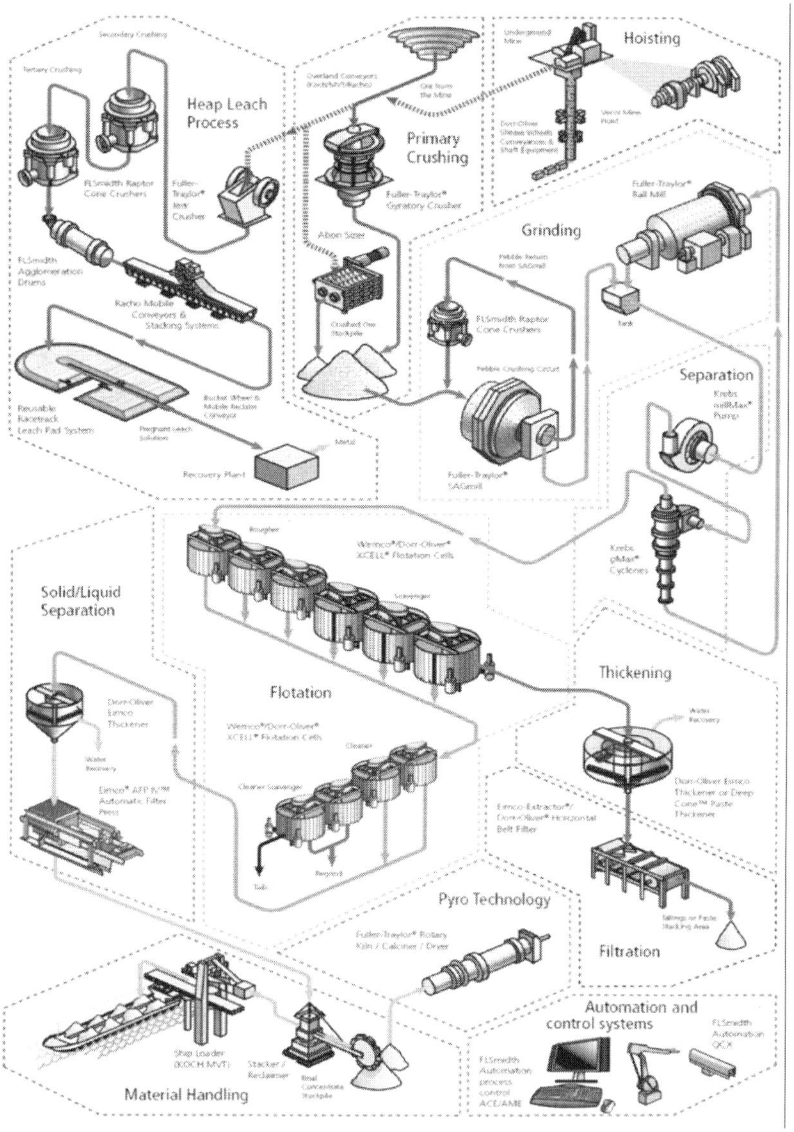

Minerals

FLSmidth

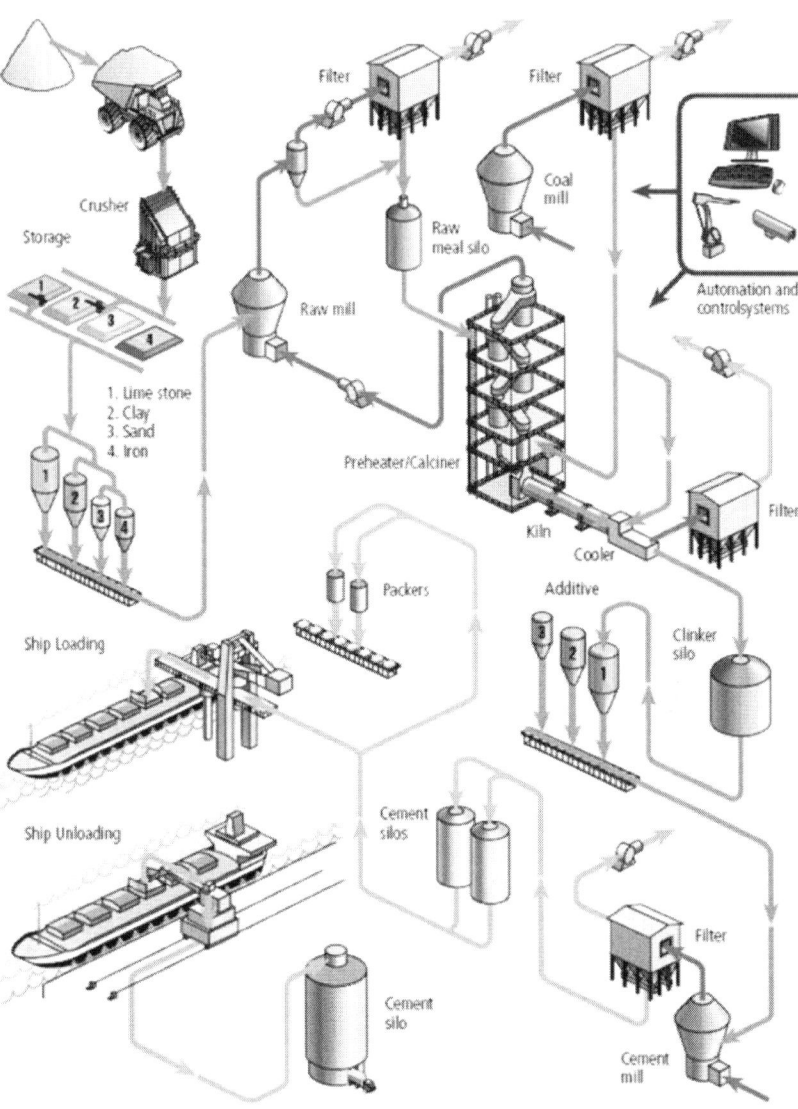

Cements

Strategies in emerging markets

Exhibit 5 – Future product mix expectations[80]

Category	Cyclical Nature	Current Share of Turnover	Expected Share of Turnover in near future
Projects	Very cyclical	Approx. 50-60%	↘
Product companies	Less cyclical	Approx. 40-50%	
Customer services	Slightly cyclical	Approx. 40-50%	↗

Exhibit 6 – Market share and peer comparison[81]

Market shares 2007 based on global contracted kiln capacity (excl. China) (in percent)

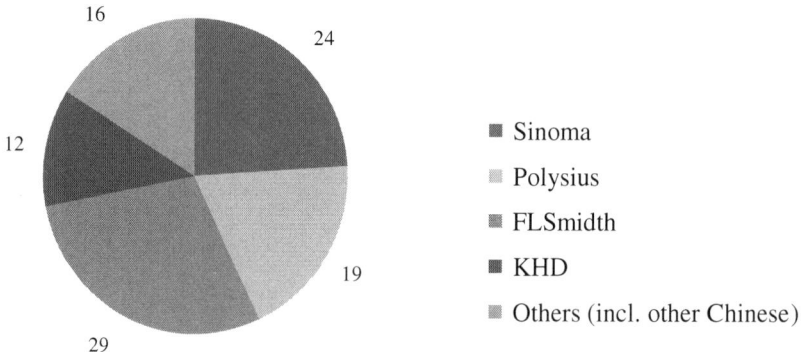

Cement Peers – Financial performance

DKKm	Market share (kiln cap. excl. China) 2007	Order intake 2007 Full year	Order intake 2008 Q1-Q3	Turnover 2007 Full year	Turnover 2008 Q1-Q3
FLSmidth Cement	29%	15,789	13,760	12,210	9,735
Sinoma	24%	17,100	n/a	8,600	6,700
Polysius	19%	n/a	n/a	n/a	n/a
KHD Cement	12%	4,810	3,070	3,160	2,000

Exhibit 7 – Overview of peer group activities[82]

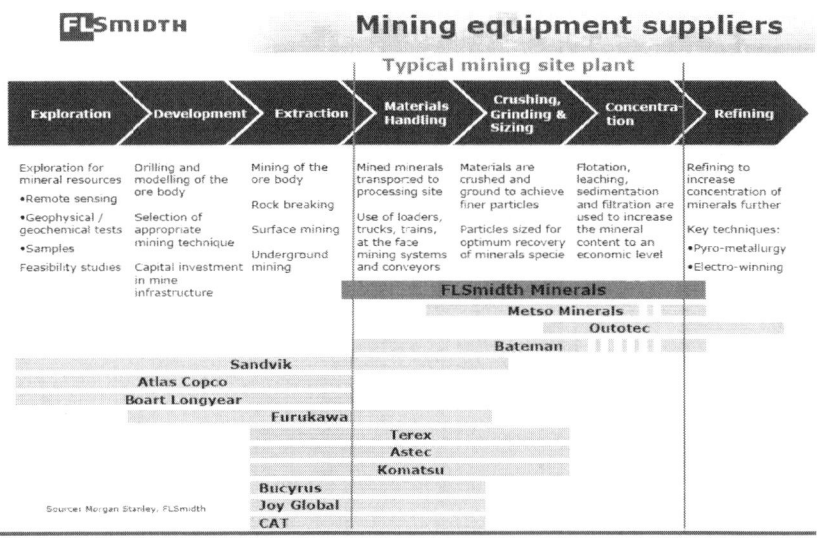

Strategies in emerging markets

Exhibit 8 – Geographical breakdown of revenue (2008)

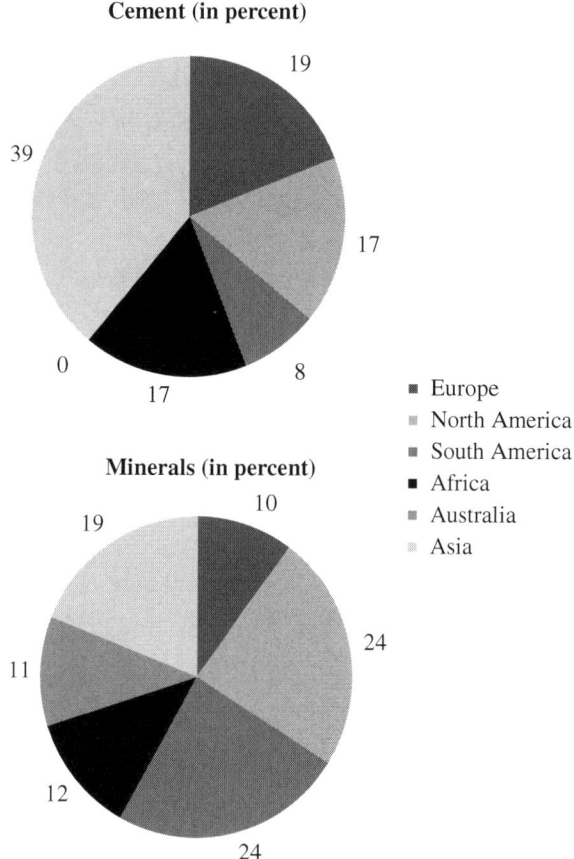

CHAPTER 5

Bestseller – Facing a new competitive landscape in China

In the fall of 1996, Bestseller became one of the first international fashion companies to enter the Chinese retail market. Earlier that year, two good friends, Allan Warburg and Dan Friis, had made contact with the CEO of Bestseller A/S, Troels Holch Povlsen, regarding prospects of selling Bestseller brands in China, where they felt there were many business opportunities. Holch Povlsen found himself believing in the two entrepreneurs and was convinced by their enthusiasm for the Chinese market. At the same time, he was in need of some help with Bestseller's purchasing offices in Hong Kong and Beijing. The plans materialized in the joint formation of Bestseller Fashion Group China Ltd. (Bestseller China), and the first outlet for the ONLY brand was established in a department store in Beijing.

Allan Warburg and Dan Friis quickly proved that they had been right about China. Within the first year, Bestseller China opened 24 stores in 9 different cities, and it introduced two other brands from Bestseller A/S's portfolio, Jack & Jones and Vero Moda, in the beginning of the new millennium. A little more than a decade after the first store opened, Bestseller China had almost 2,000 stores and had a turnover equal to more than one-third of the total turnover of Bestseller A/S. The secret to Bestseller China's extraordinary success was its ability to sell price-competitive European designs with a Chinese touch, which was achieved by locating all production in China and modifying Bestseller A/S's designs to suit the size and tastes of Chinese middle-class consumers.

With a ten-year head start over potential competitors, Bestseller China had by the end of 2007 managed to establish a strong presence in China. However, the high economic growth and the growing middle class were making the Chinese market highly attractive for other companies, a fact that Troels Holch Povlsen was very aware of: "There is a growing and reasonable market in China for many different consumer goods, but that also means that the competition is increasing",[83] he said. However, although global giants, such as Zara and H&M, were devoting big chunks of their budgets to enter China and capture market shares, these aggressive new entrants were not Holch Povlsen's biggest concern. As he saw it: "The competition that we see is not coming from American or European players, but from local companies… and in the future, we will not only see Chinese goods, but also Chinese companies on an international level – that is certain".[84]

Introducing Bestseller A/S

In 1975, Troels Holch Povlsen founded a family-owned company, Bestseller A/S, and opened his first clothing shop in Ringkøbing, Denmark. The aim of the company was to sell modern clothes of good quality at competitive prices. Some 30 years later, the focus remained the same, and Bestseller A/S had grown in line with some of its most famous brands, such as Vero Moda, Jack & Jones and ONLY, to become a large, multinational fashion company with more than 4,100 shops in 41 countries and turnover of approximately DKK 10.2 billion (EUR 1,397 million; Chinese turnover not included (Exhibit 1). The three decades of continuous growth had ensured the company a position as the industry leader in Denmark with a turnover that was nearly twice as high as turnover for its biggest Danish competitors.

According to Bestseller A/S, the company's primary goal was "to create a company that concentrates on developing people before business",[85] which was reflected in the vision of "one world – one philosophy – one family"[86] and in the company's ten basic principles, which were formulated in 1975 (see Exhibit 2). Troels Holch Povlsen emphasized the necessity of developing employees in order to develop the company. "It would sadden me if our company is judged solely on financial figures" he said. "Real life success is about well-being and personal development".[87] The basic principles included soft values, such as honesty, loyalty and cooperation, while a business mindset and a focus on results were also regarded as very important.

In 2001, Anders Holch Povlsen became co-owner of Bestseller A/S and replaced his father as CEO. Nevertheless, Troels Holch Povlsen remained a leading figure in Bestseller A/S, focusing specifically on business development and activities in emerging markets.[88]

Products and markets

Initially, the company dealt only with women's fashion but, over the years, Bestseller A/S widened its brand portfolio considerably, expanding into children's clothes, menswear and accessories. By choosing a multi-brand approach, Bestseller could build up an extensive brand portfolio, which allowed it to target different customer segments while sharing various back office functions across brands. For instance, Vero Moda targeted teenage girls and women with its "trendy and fresh style", while Jack & Jones – "cool denim fashion with an international attitude" – centered on males aged 18 to 30. ONLY, with its streetwear style, focused on younger girls "with an attitude" (see Exhibit 3). This approach meant that customers were not familiar with the company name, as the different brands were presented separately. One challenge for Bestseller A/S, therefore, was to ensure that the multi-brand strategy did not lead to brand cannibalism.

Bestseller A/S sold its products in a wide range of countries throughout the world. The Scandinavian market was considered to be the largest, although the importance of emerging markets continued to rise (see Exhibit 4). "It is difficult for us to say no to new markets. We have turned down countries, such as the US and France, but taken on less-obvious markets, such as Saudi Arabia and Russia" Troels Holch Povlsen explained. "It is an unbelievable feeling to know that our clothes are being sold in so many places in the world today. But I am proud of it". [89]

Global value chain

The internationalization and immense growth of Bestseller A/S influenced the structure of the company significantly in the sense that a large number of foreign and domestic subsidiaries were set up to handle retail, wholesale and purchasing activities (see Exhibit 5). In addition, Troels Holch Povlsen held personal ownership of a Hong Kong company as well as Bestseller Fashion Group China, which was not an integral part of Bestseller A/S. The financial results from the Chinese operations were therefore not included in the annual accounts of Bestseller A/S. Other key players, such as Anders Holch Povlsen and Managing Director Finn Poulsen, had similar personal stakes in related companies.

In the early 1980s, when Bestseller A/S went against conventional wisdom and began to move production abroad, the intention was to explore the opportunities offered by other countries. "We were not talking about outsourcing when we began to look across borders 25 years ago. We said that it was exciting to go abroad and see what we could produce there",[90] Troels Holch Povlsen recollected. Bestseller A/S specialized in the design, sales and marketing of clothes and accessories, but the company's capabilities and experience in handling outsourced production were central to its continued success. The entire production was managed through Bestseller's purchasing offices located in Italy, Turkey, China and India, while the company sourced from different suppliers in Europe, the Middle East and Asia. Tight control of the suppliers was central to the company's sourcing strategy in terms of ensuring the quality of production. In 2002, a Code of Conduct was introduced to clarify the minimum standards that Bestseller A/S expected of its suppliers and subcontractors and its expectations in relation to working conditions at the factories, social responsibility and environmental issues (see Exhibit 6).

The majority of Bestseller A/S's design and marketing activities were located

Strategies in emerging markets

in the Danish headquarters, where each brand was handled separately and some back-office functions were centralized. A multi-channel approach to distribution allowed Bestseller A/S to distribute its products through company-owned stores, wholesale operations and franchises. In fact, most of Bestseller A/S's sales took place through franchised chain stores under the brands Vero Moda, ONLY, Jack & Jones, Selected, name it and VILA. The chain stores were launched in 1988 and were based on close relationships with the franchisees, for whom Bestseller A/S was the sole supplier. Product lines were also sold through more than 12,000 independent wholesale dealers on an international scale (see Exhibit 7). The extensive sales network placed high demands on the logistical aspect of the value chain as well as on logistics management in terms of ensuring fast deliveries and small stocks while keeping costs down. These were regarded as key competitive parameters.[91]

Competitors

Bestseller A/S was by far the industry leader in Denmark with turnover nearly twice as high as the turnover of the biggest domestic competitors, IC Companys and Brandtex, which also competed in price-sensitive women's children's and men's fashion. These companies followed a multibrand strategy but they differed somewhat from Bestseller in terms of target segments. While IC Companys, with its slightly more expensive brands, such as Peak Performance, InWear and Tiger of Sweden, focused more on quality-conscious women and men, Brandtex concentrated merely on women's wear of high quality at competitive prices with brands such as Brandtex, b.young, and Fransa (see Exhibit 8). The geographical reach of Bestseller A/S was significantly wider than that of Brandtex and IC Companys. Brandtex had sales in 19 European countries, IC Companys competed across Europe, Canada and Hong Kong, while Bestseller A/S sold its clothes in 41 countries, including Canada, China, and countries in the Middle East and Europe.

As a result of the company's international presence, Bestseller needed to pay close attention to the international competitors. In fact, Troels Holch Povlsen stated that "Bestseller's best competitors are not to be found in Denmark".[92] Three large players in the fashion retail business were often mentioned: Zara (Spain), Gap Inc. (US) and H&M (Sweden). Each of these companies operated extensively on global markets and targeted the same consumers as Bestseller A/S. In terms of turnover, results and numbers of employees, the three companies exceeded Bestseller A/S by far. The Danish company could only match the international competition in relation to the number of stores (see Exhibit 9).

The geographical scope of the international competitors differed considerably. The biggest player in terms of turnover, Gap Inc. operated in the US, the UK, France and Japan, and was therefore not present in any emerging markets.

Neither was H&M, which had a strong position in Europe as well as a small presence in the US. Only Zara possessed an extensive global reach, with stores in 56 countries in Europe, the US, North Africa, Asia Pacific and the Middle East. However, most of Zara's sales were generated in the European market, and the fact that 90% of Zara's stores were located in Europe and the US revealed that the company only had a minor presence in emerging markets relative to the overall size of the firm. However, as the importance of emerging markets was growing in terms of increasing demand, the global players were starting to pay more attention to developments in these regions.

Bestseller China

In 1996, Allan Warburg and Dan Friis decided to quit their jobs at The East Asiatic Company and McKinsey & Company, respectively, to set up Bestseller Fashion Group China Ltd. (Bestseller China) together with Troels Holch Povlsen. Their ambition was to build a big company. As Warburg explained: "Going back to Denmark was not really an option, as I considered China to be my new home market. That was where the opportunity and market potential were".[93] DKK 8 million was put into the company, half of which was provided by Troels Holch Povlsen. The other half was to be provided by the two entrepreneurs, but as they were unable to raise sufficient capital on their own, the Danish Industrialization Fund for Developing Countries (IFU) participated, providing 30% of the required capital. Allan Warburg and Dan Friis each provided 10% and they also bought back the shares from IFU in 2001 (see Exhibit 10). Bestseller Fashion Group China Ltd. was registered as an independent company, separate from Bestseller A/S's outsourced clothes production in China, and it was managed by Allan Warburg and Dan Friis from an office in Beijing.

Bestseller China experienced significant growth immediately, which is particularly evident in figures related to store development (see Exhibit 11). In 1996, a few wholly owned ONLY shops were established in Beijing. Within the span of five years, Vero Moda, Jack & Jones and two other brands from Bestseller A/S portfolio had been introduced to the new market, while 163 stores were located in different cities around China. A little more than a decade after Bestseller China was founded, the company had nearly 2,000 wholly owned or franchised stores under the three brands. For Bestseller A/S's management in Denmark, the success in China came as a bit of a surprise. "It was actually a long-term investment, but I am surprised by how well it is going. There are young people who can and want to buy – and more are coming", said Finn Poulsen, co-owner and CEO of the subsidiary Bestseller Retail Denmark.[94]

The Chinese market
Between 1997 and 2003, total consumer spending in China increased by 64.2%,

while spending on clothes and footwear increased by 22%. Over the same period, per capita disposable income in China's urban areas increased by 64.2%.[95] The growing group of fashion-conscious, young consumers living in the big cities meant that Bestseller China could sell its clothes at 85% of Danish prices. Allan Warburg characterized the typical Bestseller China customer as a woman in her mid-twenties, employed in a foreign joint venture with a monthly salary of around DKK 3,000 (EUR 400)[96], of which she spent one-third on clothes and shoes. This was made possible by the fact that she had no expenses for food or rent, because she still lived with her parents. He estimated that approximately 300,000 women had sufficient purchasing power to buy ONLY or Vero Moda clothes in Beijing alone.[97]

At the time of entry, the Chinese fashion retail market was highly fragmented. Foreign luxury brands catered to the higher-price segment through outlets in upscale department stores or licensed shops,[98] and several other product markets were dominated by a few big companies. However, this was not the case for the middle-level fashion market. Bestseller China was therefore able to build an extensive sales network in a very short period of time. This meant, for instance, that the Jack & Jones brand met little competition when it was introduced in 2000: "Jack & Jones is, by far, the leader in the market because there's not so much competition for Jack & Jones. Men's wear in China is rather traditional and has not developed as much as women's wear", Warburg explained. "Sportswear for men, however, has much more competition with large companies like Nike, Adidas, Puma, Li Ning and so on, but luckily we are not in the sportswear industry".[99]

Production
The fact that Bestseller A/S already had a large sourcing operation involving Chinese suppliers was supportive for Bestseller China as it set up local production – the suppliers were more willing to cooperate despite the initially modest volumes. In the beginning, therefore, the new company benefited from Bestseller A/S's established production network. In order for the pricing strategy to work, Bestseller China's collections needed to be produced locally or the clothes would be too expensive for the middle class.

While Bestseller China's ownership structure meant that Allan Warburg and Dan Friis enjoyed a large degree of local autonomy and met with the Board of Directors only once or twice a year, the initial agreement between the three partners incorporated the purchasing offices of Bestseller A/S in Hong Kong and Beijing, which were not running properly. For Troels Holch Povlsen, the partnership created an opportunity to get help with the company's sourcing in China from two committed Danes in Beijing. In the first five years following the establishment of Bestseller China, Allan Warburg and Dan Friis assisted Bestseller A/S with the structuring of its Beijing office and set up a purchasing office in Shanghai, but a renegotiation of the shareholder agreement in 2001 meant that the two entrepreneurs could then devote their full attention to Bestseller China. Although they no longer directly assisted with the sourcing in China, the new company's continued success influenced Bestseller A/S in Europe through increased brand awareness of the Chinese suppliers. "I think being big in China helps you on the sourcing side, and that has really been the case for Bestseller", Allan Warburg argued. "All of the suppliers know the brands now. They are very serious about Bestseller products".[100]

One key aspect of Bestseller China's strategy was adaptation to local conditions. Although the concept remained the same as for Bestseller A/S and, even though Chinese stores were identical to those in the rest of the world, the actual styles and models sold in the stores were modified to match local conditions. In this regard, Warburg stated that "Chinese women have a different figure than women in the Western world. They are much more slender. And they typically dress in a more feminine way than Western women. Our products should reflect that".[101] Colors were also changed to fit the Chinese taste, so that, for instance, all military coloring was left out. In order to adapt the product range, the designs for each brand were sent from Denmark to a Danish designer located in China who was in charge of modifying them together with a team of Chinese designers. This process meant that Bestseller China employed three Danes in addition to Allan Warburg and Dan Friis. The key to Bestseller China's success was the European style of the products, which also explained the composition of the design team. "The only thing that we haven't wanted or been able to localize in the design process is the fact that each of the brands has one Danish designer", said Mr. Warburg. "What we are selling is a European lifestyle".[102] The overall Western style of the designs from Bestseller A/S was therefore maintained, while the clothes were fine-tuned to better fit the Chinese consumers.

When asked to suggest reasons for the immense success of Bestseller China, Allan Warburg pointed to the location and value-chain configuration of the company. "You've got to localize everything here in China", he argued. "We have seen so many of our competitors from Europe coming in, starting up and then two years later, pulling out again. The reason is that they are sitting in Europe and trying to manage China. We are sitting in China, producing 100% of our products for the Chinese market in China".[103]

Marketing and distribution
A multi-channel approach, similar to the approach employed by Bestseller A/S, was used for the Chinese market. The sales network consisted of a mixture of franchises and wholly-owned stores, with the long-term aim of eventually making franchising the main approach. The franchising concept had been

introduced slowly, as it was relatively new when Bestseller China entered the market in 1996. In 2005, approximately half of Bestseller China's stores were franchised in cities the two entrepreneurs did not want to enter, while the other half were owned by the company. All product purchasing was handled by the main office in Beijing, from which products were subsequently distributed to the different branch offices, which only concentrated on the sales in their respective areas. Furthermore, Bestseller China had three flagship stores, located in Beijing, Shanghai and Tianjin, which were of great importance in building brand recognition. Although they were located in prestigious shopping malls where rents were so high that earnings were limited, the flagship stores were central to Bestseller China's strategy, as being in close proximity to other international brands helped Bestseller China build its own brands. For instance, for the company's store in Guo Mao, one of Beijing's high-end shopping malls, expenses were actually higher than they would be for a similar store in Europe. As Friis said: "The high rent limits our profits at this location. But it is important that we are here to build up our brands. All of the big international brands are here – and many of them are running with a huge deficit on their stores... We do not have that".[104]

Other central elements of the company's marketing efforts comprised aggressive advertising in Chinese magazines and big posters featuring, for instance, Danish supermodel Helena Christensen, who represented northern European culture. The German supermodel Claudia Schiffer was another important face for Bestseller China's brands, whose well-known look further emphasized the European image. Moreover, Bestseller China's marketing comprised fashion shows in night clubs and smaller, creative initiatives, such as the featuring of ONLY and Jack & Jones logos on tablecloths in Starbucks cafés and in restaurants. However, although a great deal of energy was used on branding through various marketing channels, the stores were considered most important. "We actually spend money on fashion magazines and also on fashion shows, but I think the most important way we build our brand is actually through the shops", Warburg explained. "Shops are where you build your image because customers are out shopping anyway and they walk by and see our shops. That's where we build our brand, much more than in any other ways".[105]

The competitive challenges facing Bestseller China
Global competitors in China
Given China's increased economic growth and growing middle class, competition from large global fashion companies started to increase. The Swedish giant H&M, for instance, opened its first Chinese store in 2007, aimed at obtaining a share of the booming fashion market. "We are growing by 10% to 15% annually and we open 180 stores a year. We started in the US in 2000 and that has

been sufficient to fulfill our own demands. However, for the future, it is most important that we enter the Chinese market",[106] commented CEO Rolf Eriksen in connection with the opening of the first Chinese H&M store. The company used two years to prepare for its market entry and concluded that there was no need to customize the sizes and styles of the company's collections to the Chinese consumers. Accordingly, 80% of the clothes in the new H&M store were similar to the collections in the European and North American stores. The company entered China convinced that good PR, based on relationships with famous celebrities, such as Madonna, Kylie Minogue and Karl Lagerfeld, in conjunction with its famous collection would suffice. Spanish Zara also showed a particular interest in the Chinese consumers. With 15 Chinese stores in 2008, Zara pursued a strategy of using globally standardized collections in its Chinese stores. Furthermore, it was rumored that Gap Inc. would also enter the Chinese market at some point.

Operating with a significantly smaller budget, IC Companys once again tried to enter the Chinese market in 2005. This time, the company tried to copy Bestseller China's strategy of local adaptation and the firm aligned itself with a Chinese marketing bureau. IC Companys' Export Director Steen Petersen said: "We have prepared ourselves for this. We have studied competitors and looked over their shoulders. Both Esprit and Bestseller have great success in China, so it is obvious that we could learn something from them".[107] For instance, IC Companys aimed to produce all of its clothes in China, thereby keeping prices low for the middle class and it customized its collections to suit Chinese consumers.

Dan Friis commented on the potential for increased competition from global companies: "We are very positive towards our new professional 'colleagues'. Many shopping malls have failed as there were not enough professional brands to open large stores with the management and products needed to attract a larger customer base. That is going to happen now".[108] However, after Bestseller China's establishment in 1996, the market had become increasingly difficult to penetrate. For instance, marketing costs had increased significantly and the number of foreign operators had exploded after China fully joined the WTO in 2001. "Being early in China definitely had many advantages, as the speed was slower and you didn't have to invest that much money at that time", said Allan Warburg.[109]

Local competition
From their headquarters in Hong Kong, an increasing number of strong local brands were beginning to look towards mainland China for new market opportunities. Although they were not that well known internationally, these brands had established themselves on a regional scale. Clothing from Hong Kong was perceived by customers in mainland China to offer good design and quality. Hong

Strategies in emerging markets

Kong's clothing industry had undergone a transformation since the first companies started manufacturing there in the 1950s when labor costs were low. As the producers became more sophisticated and prices increased, Hong Kong had lost its comparative cost advantage to other countries, including China, and own equipment manufacturing (OEM) was no longer sufficient. In order to remain competitive, the industry began to focus on own design manufacturing (ODM), which meant that buyers could either use the designs of the Hong Kong companies as they were or modify them to fit their own particular needs. Although ODM prevailed in the 1990s, it was evident at the beginning of the new millennium that higher profits could be obtained through own brand manufacturing (OBM). In fact, some estimated the profit margins of OBM to be 50% higher than ODM.[110] This led a number of Hong Kong companies, such as Bossini International Holdings Ltd. and The Giordano Group, to brand their own designs in the pursuit of high revenues. While the developed markets were hard to penetrate for these companies, they could see many opportunities in the mainland's mid-market segment due to the absence of global brands. They therefore also decided to enter China.

By the end of 2007, Bossini had opened 551 Chinese outlets, which made up more than half of the company's global distribution network. 827 of Giordano's 1,800 shops were located in China. Another important competitor was the medium sized player Esprit, which originated from the US but had relocated its headquarters and creative offices to Hong Kong. In order to accommodate the growing fashion-conscious middle class in China, which had a preference for European style, Esprit decided to modify only 20-30% of its products to suit the Chinese market. The remaining products were similar to the products sold in the rest of the world. While Esprit was already a global player, the two other companies aspired to a global presence and were already serving many markets across the globe. In fact, Giordano's vision was "to be the best and the biggest world brand in apparel retailing".[111] For Bestseller China, which dominated the mid-market, this development meant that Allan Warburg and Dan Friis not only had to defend their market position against global entrants, but they also had to keep a close eye on new competitors from Hong Kong.

Nevertheless, in the eyes of Allan Warburg, these companies did not pose the biggest threat to Bestseller China's market position. "A lot of the Hong Kong brands have not been able to make it here", he said. "They're big in Hong Kong. They've tried to establish themselves in China, but they've never made it".[112] He explained the failure by referring to the fact that although these companies had production located in China, they managed all of their operations from offices in Hong Kong and could not, therefore, move as fast as Bestseller China.

However, the story was different for companies from mainland China. "There are some very good local Chinese companies out there at the moment, who are operating at a lower price margin", said Warburg.[113] Over the years, China had built a strong position worldwide as a textile manufacturer and, as a result, the "made in China" label was generally associated with cheap production. Low unit costs meant that the industry had attracted the sourcing activities of a large number of foreign companies, but China's population size and vast income disparities had made it difficult for local companies to build their own brands. However, given diminishing profit margins in production, it was unclear whether this component of the value chain would be sufficient for the future. "I think our main competitors in the future will be local Chinese companies", Allan Warburg declared. "They are already starting up their businesses and they will most likely become bigger as they expand by setting up design offices in Europe and in the US. They can keep costs to a minimum, as they will have most of their expenses in China".[114]

* * *

Troels Holch Povlsen and his two partners, Dan Friis and Allan Warburg, had clearly enjoyed the benefits of entering China as early as 1996. With high consumer awareness of all three brands and almost 2,000 shops, the success of Bestseller China was unmistakable. In fact, a decade after the establishment of the company, the Chinese activities were estimated to constitute more than one-third of Bestseller's total turnover. However, the large global players were eager to challenge Bestseller China in an attempt to grab a share of the booming Chinese retail market. In addition, Warburg and Friis were keeping an eye on the new Chinese firms, which they felt could pose a significant threat to their market position. The ten-year head start had evidently provided a number of significant advantages, but it was uncertain whether the organizational setup of Bestseller China and Bestseller A/S provided the company with the best possible foundation for fending off new competitors and sustaining its position as market leader in the booming Chinese fashion retail market.

Exhibits for Bestseller A/S case

Bestseller

Exhibit 1 – Bestseller A/S' key figures[115]

	2003	2004	2005	2006	2007
Profit and loss account (million DKK)					
Turnover	4,924	5,336	6,713	8,672	10,182
Turnover Europe	4,881	5,272	6,516	8,305	9,722
Turnover rest of the world	43	64	197	367	460
Profit before taxation	997	875	1,316	1,497	1,869
Profit for the year	685	597	939	1,055	1,372
Equity	1,287	1,527	1,869	2,505	3,091
Balance sheet total	2,829	2,888	3,794	4,390	5,452
Key ratios					
Profit margin, %	19.4	18.7	18.7	16.0	17.2
Return on assets, %	33.8	28.9	33.0	31.7	32.2
Return on equity, %	67.5	46.3	61.5	56.5	54.8
Solvency ratio, %	45.5	52.9	49.3	57.1	56.7
Employees	1,285	1,819	2,372	2,950	4,108

Strategies in emerging markets

Exhibit 2 – Bestseller's vision and 10 basic principles[116]

One World
Our world is built on fairness and opportunities. Cultural differences are an advantage, which will promote quality, extraordinary results and good values. Always trying to give more than we promise we try to meet remoteness with closeness.

One Philosophy
We make Bestseller's 10 Basic Principles come alive. We are humble and together we work hard. We base our co-operation on trust, partnership and honesty. We treat all people as individuals but we think and act as a team. Therefore we succeed.

One Family
The backbone of Bestseller is our family feeling. We help each other and have unlimited faith in our relatives. We show our identity in the good examples we set for one another. We are proud of our family. It is both our link to the past and the foundation of our future.

10 basic principles[117]
1. We are honest
2. We are hard-working
3. We are loyal
4. We are co-operative
5. We are business minded
6. We want to see results
7. We want simple solutions
8. We take nothing for granted
9. We always keep our promises
10. We want to be the best

Exhibit 3 – Brand portfolio of Bestseller A/S[118]

Brand	Target group	Product offer	Pricing	Style	Year
EXIT	Boys and girls, ages 2-10	Full wardrobe. Underwear, regular clothing, outerwear and shoes	Jeans: EUR 20-30 Tops: EUR 13-18	Cool and fun, but functional and wearable	1986
Vero Moda	Teenagers and women	Skirts, tops, trousers, outerwear, some accessories and footwear	Dresses: EUR 35-50 Tops: €EUR 17-25	Trendy and fresh	1987
Jack & Jones	Men, ages 18-30	Jeans at the core, wide range of matching items, shoes and accessories	Trousers: EUR 40-60 T-shirts: EUR 15-25	Cool denim fashion with an international attitude	1990
Vila	Women, ages 25+	Tailored/elegant wear, some outerwear	Dresses: EUR 40-60 Jeans: €EUR 50-60	Feminine and elegant, highly fashionable	1993
name it (formerly known as EXIT)	Boys and girls, ages 0-3	Tops, trousers, dresses seasonal items (swimwear)	Tops: EUR 10 Trousers: EUR 15	Functional daywear	1996
ONLY	Girls with attitude	Jeans at the core, wide range of matching casual items	n.a.	Cool, streetwear-oriented, up-to-date, trendy	1996
Selected	Men, ages 20-35	Clean-cut design, leisure to formal wear	n.a.	Leading trends, simple and stylish	1997
Tdk	Young men	Jeans and trend items	n.a.	Jeans from casual to innovative/unique	1999
PH industries	Boys, ages 8-16	Jeans, t-shirts, knits, sweaters, outerwear	Jeans: EUR 20-35 Sweatshirts: EUR 15-35	Fresh everyday wear, focus on comfort and functionality	1999
phink industries	Girls, ages 8-16	Jeans and matching items, outerwear	Jeans: EUR 20-45, Shirts: EUR 25-30	Trendy with a casual or urban edge	2003
Object Collectors Item	Girls with attitude	An ONLY sub-brand, jeans and streetwear	n.a.	Cool styles with high design	2003
Pieces accessories	Women	Hosiery, bikinis, belts, bags, footwear, jewelry	n.a.	Designed for the urban fashionistas	2003
Gosha by Vero Moda	Women	Luxury women's wear (at Vero Moda stores)	n.a.	Elegant, refined, high-quality fashion	2005
mama-licious	Expectant mothers	Trousers, skirts, tops	Skirts: EUR 30-40 Jeans: EUR 45-75	Trendy, sexy, glamorous	2005
Outfitters Nation	Unisex teens	Jeanswear, sportswear, feminine dresses and outdoor clothing	n.a.	Trendy cool teen styles	2007

Strategies in emerging markets

Exhibit 4 – Bestseller A/S European and non-European outlets, September 2007[119]

	Jack & Jones	Vero Moda	ONLY	EXIT	Vila	Selected	Pieces	Other	Total
Austria	7	16	4	3				1	31
Belgium	9	19	5						33
Croatia	2	2							4
Cyprus		1							1
Czech Republic		3	1						4
Denmark	46	67	37	27	32	9	7	16	241
Estonia	1	2			1				4
Finland	22	26	9	2	7		1		67
Germany	46	80	23	2			1		152
Iceland	2	2	1	2	1			1	9
Ireland	19	19	1	11	4				54
Latvia	1	1	1						3
Lithuania		6	2						8
Luxembourg	1	1							2
Netherlands	57	75	39	4	13	4	7		199
Norway	65	72	26	21	10	5		1	200
Poland	10	23						4	37
Russia	6	6							12
Slovakia	3	1	1						5
Slovenia		3							3
Spain	58	10	5	1		14			88
Sweden	45	71	10	20	23	1			170
Switzerland	4	24	1						29
UK	13	4	1		2				20
Total	417	534	167	93	93	33	16	23	1,376

	Jack & Jones	Vero Moda	EXIT	ONLY	Total
Bahrain	1	1		1	3
Egypt	1	1	1		3
Jordan			1		1
Lebanon	3	4	5		12
Qatar		1			1
Saudi Arabia	2	5	6		13
Syria	1	1			2
Turkey	3	3			6
UAE	3	3			6
Total of above	14	19	13	1	47

Bestseller

Exhibit 5 – Organizational structure, Bestseller A/S, 2007[120]

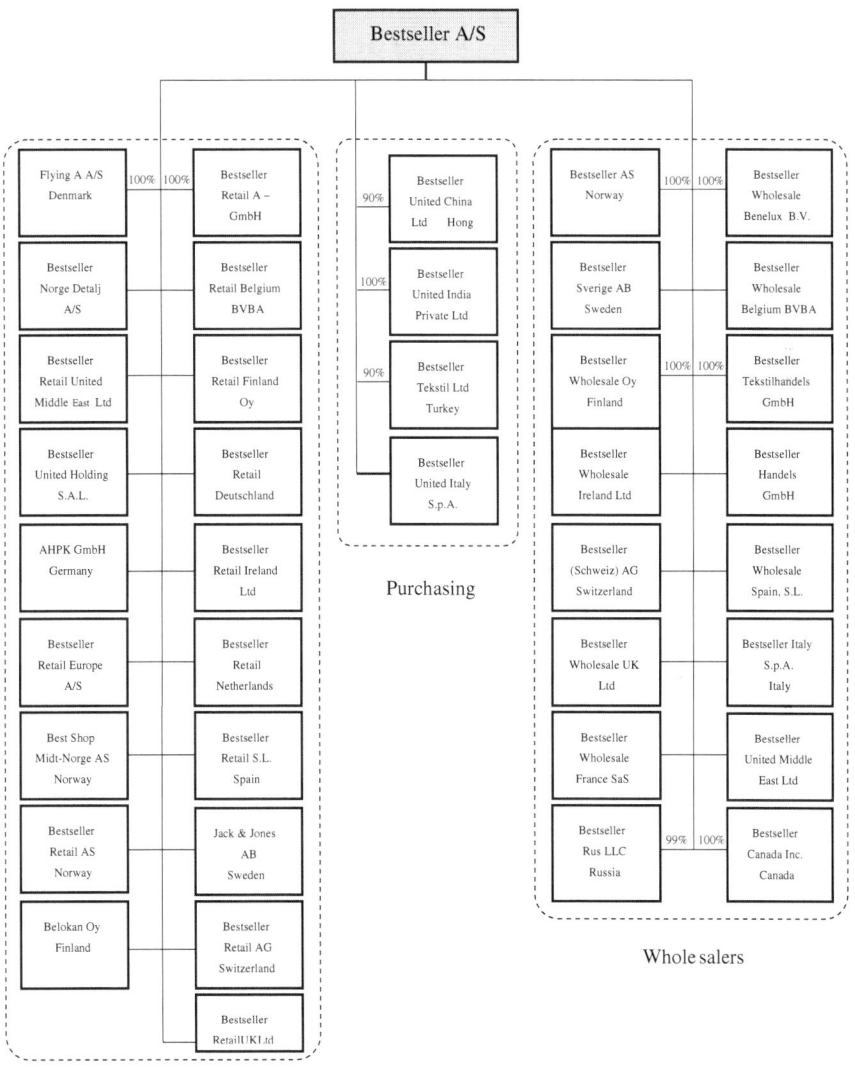

Strategies in emerging markets

Exhibit 6 – Bestseller A/S Code of Conduct – General Principles[121]

0.1.0 This Code of Conduct describes the ethics that Bestseller wishes to promote. It is based on a fundamental attitude of Bestseller: "We do what we say and we keep our promises."

* * *

0.2.0 The Code of Conduct is directed at any supplier and his subcontractors, who manufacture products for Bestseller A/S or for any of Bestseller's companies.

Bestseller must be informed about all sub-contractors producing Bestseller's orders.

The supplier is responsible for the communication of this Code of Conduct to his sub-contractors.

Suppliers including their subcontractors will hereinafter be called "the suppliers".

0.1.1. Any supplier shall observe the legislation in force at the time in question. This includes an obligation to observe and comply with all EU product requirements at the time in question.

0.1.2. Even though Bestseller acknowledges that legislation and cultural patterns vary across the world and that suppliers consequently operate under different circumstances, this Code of Conduct sets out the basic requirements that any supplier must comply with in order to do business with Bestseller.

In cases where the law in question is more comprehensive than this Code of Conduct, current law applies. In cases where this Code of Conduct is more comprehensive than the law in question, this Code of Conduct applies.

0.1.3 Code of Conduct also forms the basis upon which Bestseller will make a continuous evaluation of the supplier's compliance with Bestseller's requirements and expectations.

* * *

0.3.0 It is a prerequisite for doing business with Bestseller that any supplier complies with the Code of Conduct.

Bestseller will constantly develop its follow-up system regarding evaluation and compliance with the Code of Conduct.

Bestseller

0.3.1 If a supplier is not in full compliance with this Code of Conduct, Bestseller is entitled to demand that the supplier implements a development plan to remedy the deficiencies.

0.3.2 If Bestseller has recommended such a development plan, and it is not implemented, Bestseller is entitled to without any notice to terminate its business relation and possibly cancel any production or delivery in progress.

0.3.3 A serious violation of Bestseller's Code of Conduct can lead to an immediate determination of the cooperation.

* * *

0.4.0 The specific requirements in this Code of Conduct are listed under the following headings:
2.0.0 The Working Environment and Housing Conditions
3.0.0 Social Responsibility
4.0.0 Environmentally Friendly Production
5.0.0 Protection of Animals

* * *

0.5.0 Suppliers who deliver and/or manufacture products for Bestseller A/S shall operate in compliance with the laws and regulations that apply in their respective countries and in compliance with this Code of Conduct, i.e.:

0.5.1 The supplier shall treat both people and animals with respect and dignity. The supplier shall treat the environment with respect and consideration.

0.5.2 The supplier's business activities must comply with all the relevant and applicable laws and regulations including those concerning the workforce, its welfare and safety and the working environment.

0.5.3 The supplier shall allow Bestseller A/S and/or anyone who represents Bestseller free access to his facilities (incl sub-contractor's facilities) and employees and to all the relevant data at any time, whether notification of an audit has been given in advance or not.

* * *

1.6.0 The supplier shall ensure that the content of this Code of Conduct is communicated to the employees including posting a copy of the Code of Conduct in the local language and in a place accessible to the employees.

Strategies in emerging markets

Exhibit 7 – Global Value Chain, Bestseller A/S[122]

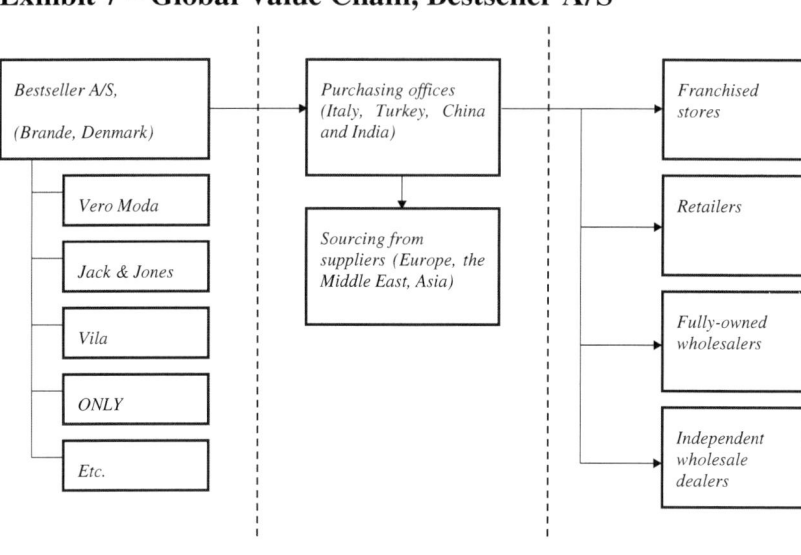

Exhibit 8 – Bestseller A/S's Danish competitors

Key figures, 2003-2007[123]

	2003	2004	2005	2006	2007
IC Companys					
Turnover (DKK mill.)	2,706	2,612	2,819	3,022	3,354
Net earnings (DKK mill.)	1	-309	173	224	241
Employees	2,199	2,095	2,019	1,989	2,199
Brandtex					
Turnover (DKK mill.)	3,048	3,282	3,371	3,369	3,194
Net earnings (DKK mill.)	74	68	46	29	72
Employees	2,397	2,360	1,871	1,752	1,593
Bestseller					
Turnover (DKK mill.)	4,924	5,336	6,713	8,672	10,182
Net earnings (DKK mill.)	685	597	939	1,055	1,372
Employees	1,285	1,819	2,372	2,950	4,108

IC Companys brands:[124] Peak Performance, InWear, Jackpot, Tiger of Sweden, Cottonfield, Matinique, Part Two, Saint Tropez, By Malene Birger, Soaked in Luxury and Designers Remix Collection

Brandtex brands:[125] Brandtex, SHARE, Ciso, Blend, BlendShe, b.young, Fransa, Edamae, Psycho Cowboy, Jensen Women, Gestuz, Freeze, Ichi, Silbor, Veto, Frank Q, Dranella, Signature

Strategies in emerging markets

Exhibit 9 – Bestseller A/S's international competitors[126]

Key figures, 2003-2007					
	2003	2004	2005	2006	2007
Gap Inc.[127]					
Net sales (USD mill.)	15,854	16,267	16,019	15,923	15,763
Net earnings (USD mill.)	1,031	1,150	1,113	778	833
Employees	153,000	152,000	153,000	154,000	150,000
H&M[128]					
Net sales (USD mill.)	9,413	10,485	11,966	13,330	15,335
Net earnings (USD mill.)	1,063	1,211	1,539	1,797	2,262
Employees	28,409	31,701	34,614	40,368	47,029
Zara[129]					
Net sales (USD mill.)	7,219	8,742	10,582	13,996	14,810
Net earnings (USD mill.)	702	1003	1261	1573	1962
Employees	39,760	47,046	58,190	69,240	79,517
Bestseller[130]					
Net sales (USD mill.)	1,036	1,123	1,412	1,824	2,142
Net earnings (USD mill.)	144	126	198	222	289
Employees	1,285	1,819	2,372	2,950	4,108

Store locations			
	Gap Inc.	H&M	Zara
Europe	176	1,383	1,140
America	2,869	192	154
Asia-Pacific	132	7	78
Middle East	0	12	54
Africa	0	0	5
Total	3,177	1,594	1,431

Exhibit 10 – Bestseller China's ownership structure[131]

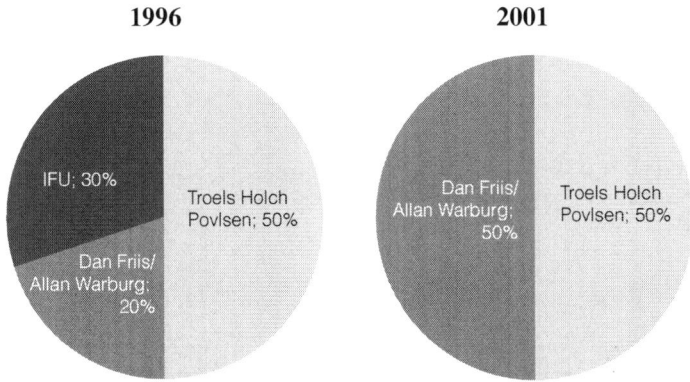

Exhibit 11
– Bestseller China's store development, 1996-2007[132, 133]

	1996	1997	1998	1999	2000	2001	2002	2003	2004	2005	2006	2007
Stores	3	24	45	56	82	163	282	484	710	852	1200	1800
Own stores	3	16	23	26	48	55	175	274	357	412	675	960
Franchises	0	8	22	30	24	108	107	210	353	440	525	840

CHAPTER 6

A.P. Møller Mærsk – Leveraging first-mover advantages in Vietnam

Standing on the dock of Cai Mep, roughly an hour south of Ho Chi Minh City in southern Vietnam, Thomas Ørting Jørgensen, A.P. Møller – Mærsk's Regional Line Manager for southeast Asia, eagerly told the Vietnamese state officials that "we in Mærsk see Vietnam as having a large, untapped potential."[134] It was here, where the majestic Mekong River met the South China Sea, that the Danish conglomerate had earlier in 2006 commenced the construction of a new DKK 1 billion deepwater terminal. Jørgensen stated that "through its geographic position, the country has also an important potential competitive advantage if investments are made in port facilities that can handle the big ships".[135] The new terminal, which would be fully operative in 2010, was the result of a joint venture between the A.P. Møller – Mærsk company, APM Terminals, the Port of Saigon and Vietnam National Shipping Lines.

Vietnam was indeed a country of growing importance for A.P. Møller – Mærsk's container shipping activities. Since the Communist Party of Vietnam's Sixth Party Congress in 1986 introduced the comprehensive economic reform package called *Đôi mói* ("economic renovation"), which emphasized a socialist-oriented market economy and, thereby, the displacement of the centrally planned economy, the southeast Asian country has witnessed average annual GDP growth of 7-8%, making it the second-fastest growing economy in the world. The number of registered companies had increased from 14,000 in 1990 to almost one million in 2006, and the figure now included a significant portion of foreign-owned companies. The demand for overseas shipping had correspondingly increased sharply.

A.P. Møller – Mærsk's Vietnamese experience dated back to 1991 when it opened a representation office. It was the first and only foreign transportation company allowed to operate in the Communist country. Two years later, the company acquired East Asiatic Company's container liner traffic and gained further access to the Vietnamese transportation market, from which it developed its container traffic from two inter-Asia lines to container liner services that

Strategies in emerging markets

spanned the globe. Prior to A.P. Møller – Mærsk's operations in Vietnam, the country had relied on general cargo and bulk technologies, and was cut off from the international container transport network. Thus, as the largest container traffic operator in the country, the Danish company carried out the important task of providing container shipping capacity for the rapidly growing Vietnamese economy. At the same time, A.P. Møller – Mærsk's entrance into Vietnam at the early stage of its economic development had ensured close relations with customers and important ties to the authorities.

However, given the booming Vietnamese economy and the liberalization of the market, mounting competition from domestic and foreign actors was unavoidable. The substantial amounts of capital tied up in large Vietnamese investments, moreover, made A.P. Møller – Mærsk increasingly prone to external chocks, such as economic crises and unfavorable policies. Escorting the Vietnamese state officials from the Cap Mei terminal construction site, Thomas Ørting Jørgensen knew he ran an entity of central importance to the Danish group. However, despite A.P. Møller – Mærsk's strength in Vietnam due to its early entrance, he was well aware that times were changing. A thorough assessment of the company's strategic position was in order if the company was going to cope with the challenges of tomorrow.

A.P. Møller – Mærsk: a Danish conglomerate

A.P. Møller – Mærsk's roots date back to 1904, when a small shipping company was founded by Peter Mærsk Møller and his son Arnold Peter Møller in Svendborg, Denmark. Following the death of A. P. Møller, his son, Arnold Mærsk McKinney Møller, became CEO, a position he held until 1993. Over a span of roughly 100 years, the company grew into a global conglomerate, operating in 130 countries with diversified business activities in container shipping, energy, shipping and offshore, energy, retail and other businesses (see Exhibit 1). This conglomeration was viewed as an advantage: "As a corporate company, A.P. Møller – Mærsk has a solid financial background," a manager in the company's southeast Asian area said. "With the size of our container business, our profitable oil activities, the supermarkets, etc., we are highly solvent. Our diversification and size allow us to make investments and self-finance a number of initiatives that benefit our customers, us and society at large".[136]

Under the motto "No loss should hit us which can be avoided with constant care", the group's consolidated revenue reached DKK 260,134 million in 2006 with profits of DKK 16,055 million (see Exhibit 2). These figures meant that A.P. Møller – Mærsk was the largest company in Denmark by far. With around 120,000 employees spread out across approximately 1,100 companies, A.P. Møller – Mærsk was ranked 161 on the Fortune Global 500 list for 2006, compared to 189 in 2005.

A.P. Møller Mærsk

The keystone of A.P. Møller – Mærsk:
Container shipping and related activities
Although A.P. Møller – Mærsk possessed a broad portfolio of activities, container shipping remained the group's core business area, constituting DKK 150,312 million in revenue, or 57.8% of the group's total, in 2008 (see Exhibit 3). The container shipping business encompassed independent units arranged along three pillars: Maersk Line/Safmarine, Maersk Logistics, and APM Terminals (see Exhibit 4). Although they were highly complementary, all of the business units operated as independent firms that interacted with each other on market terms, and they were evaluated as separate profit and loss centers.

Maersk Line and Safmarine represented the group's ocean container transport activities. Maersk Line was, in fact, the world's largest container shipping operator. By 2006, its fleet capacity was 1.46 million TEU (twenty-foot equivalent units), representing 18.8% of the world's total container capacity. From Maersk Line's establishment in 1928, its shipping network had grown to cover the entire globe with strategic centers concentrated on the main trading lines of the Europe-Far East, Transatlantic and Transpacific routes. In addition to ocean container transport, Maersk Line also provided inland haulage, in which feeder vessels, trucks and trains facilitated door-to-door transportation service. The company was divided into 17 geographical areas, and the overall business strategy was developed at A.P. Møller – Mærsk's corporate headquarters in Copenhagen. The customer portfolio included more than 100,000 customers, and could be divided into three general segments: global key clients were typically large MNCs, such as Nestlé, Wal-Mart, Nike and IKEA, which sought services on a global scale; area key clients, which had a regional origin and presence; and direct sales clients, which were global and local customers, usually shipping lower-value added commodities or located in trade corridors where Maersk Line did not have key strategic positions.

Safmarine, originally named South African Marine Corporation Limited, was an independently managed shipping company that focused primarily on container transportation to and from Africa. In 1999, A.P. Møller – Mærsk acquired Safmarine's liner shipping business as well as its trading name. It transported approximately 1,120,000 TEU in 2006.

Maersk Logistics offered forwarding services – i.e., ocean freight, airfreight and land freight – as well as global supply chain management solutions. The latter entailed import and export logistics, warehousing and distribution, supply chain development, information management, and monitoring performance. Maersk Logistics was established in 1977 (under the name of Mercantile) as a natural spin-off of A.P. Møller – Mærsk's ocean freight business, as there was a growing demand for specialized consolidation of cargo in order to better utilize container space. By 2006, the company had over 200 offices in 90 countries and

Strategies in emerging markets

was, consequently, one of the world's leading providers of integrated logistical solutions.

APM Terminals represented A.P. Møller – Mærsk's business of developing and operating container terminals. In 2006, it had 18,000 employees globally and was engaged in more than 45 terminals and terminal projects in 25 countries (see Exhibit 5). In addition to operating and managing container terminals, the company handled stevedoring, free trade zone development, port authority responsibilities and various other value-added activities. Maersk Line was by far the most important customer, accounting for 62% of APM Terminal's total volume of handled containers in 2006, measured in crane lifts and weighted by its ownership share – approximately 17.6 million TEU. The remaining 38% – 10.8 million TEU – was divided among as many as 60 other clients.

Central to APM Terminals was its investment strategy, which was based on expectations for future container port development. With container traffic growing at twice the speed of global container port capacity, one major constraint on the shipping industry was the lack of port capacity. For that reason, APM Terminals initiated an additional 11 terminal expansion projects and 12 new port projects in 2006. These were directed at developing countries in particular. For instance, concession agreements were concluded for Cai Mep in Vietnam and Aqeba in Jordan. In addition, APM Terminals took over the operation of container terminals in the ports of Apapa in Nigeria and Kahlifa Bin Salman in Bahrain, and its new container terminal in Mumbai, India welcomed its first vessels. The company was, therefore, one of the fastest growing container terminal operators in the world.

Commenting on the development of the container shipping industry, one APM terminal manager based in Singapore said: "The transport industry has undergone dramatic change over recent decades, so that transportation per unit is negligible. This trend has been driven by increasing containerization, increases in vessel size, and development of large container terminal facilities equipped with new, modern, and fast equipment and information systems, which can facilitate turnover of huge volumes in a short time. In other words, our business is driven by economies of scale, which benefits exporters in producing countries to bring their goods to the market, and enable consumers fast and cheap access to consumer goods".[137]

Creating a global market playground for MNCs

"We at A.P. Møller – Mærsk have the organizational and financial strength to set up organizations in all these Southeast Asian countries that will allow us to pursue business opportunities and develop infrastructure," expressed an A.P. Møller – Mærsk manager in Singapore, "and we have within the company over the years build a lot of competences in operating in what other people would call more difficult locations – we are both global and local".[138] Given the rapid growth in global trade that the world had experienced in recent decades, the need for actors to undertake direct and indirect exchanges among international customers had grown remarkably. In this respect, the transportation industry had played a significant role in ensuring that MNCs could efficiently source production and other value-chain activities around the whole world.

However, in contrast to most of its competitors, A.P. Møller – Mærsk's adopted an early entry-strategy aimed at "difficult" locations with significant state bureaucracies or a lack of basic infrastructure. This could, for instance, be seen in its many encounters with African and Asian countries. Freight costs in developing countries averaged 8% of the total value of imports – moving as high as 20% to 40% in some cases. The comparable level of only 4% in developed countries made this a relevant activity. "Operating in developing countries is often more motivating," an A.P. Møller – Mærsk manager said, "because the difference you make to a society is much greater, much more significant, and more measurable than in developed countries".[139] This signified that A.P. Møller – Mærsk was a truly global player that serviced multinational clients in both developed and developing countries.

The manner in which A.P. Møller – Mærsk ensured a truly global playground for its MNC clients was more evident in its large-scale investments in designing and building state-of-the-art container transport infrastructure, and in its integrated, coordinated globalized production processes. In 2005 alone, the company invested USD 5.7 billion in global container shipping, including investments in container ships, containers, container terminals and organizational expansion. Maersk Line, for instance, operated the world's largest fleet. In 2006, it acquired 17 new container vessels and 80,000 containers. It also had the world's most technologically sophisticated fleet, which facilitated faster and cheaper transport, and made it possible to trade more complicated goods. Moreover, Maersk Line was one of the few carriers in the world that was able to operate a full global route network and to provide efficient round-the-world (RTW) services. In the RTW concept, the major trans-oceanic trade routes were connected by a complete globe-encircling network moving in either an eastbound or westbound direction. Major regional ports (such as Singapore and Rotterdam) were strategically located along these routes. Cargo from intermediate locations, like Vietnam, were transshipped to the major ports. Those locations were, therefore, also connected to trans-oceanic trade routes.

Through APM Terminals, A.P. Møller – Mærsk also carried out large-scale investments in state-of-the-art container terminals to match the global growth in containerized cargo. "We do not comment on market rumors," stated an APM Terminals International B.V. manager based in Singapore, "but APM Terminals' strategy involves a significant investment program to keep pace with global

Strategies in emerging markets

growth in the container trade, to create new capacities and to alleviate bottlenecks in support of Maersk Line's and other customers' growth".[140] The geographic locations of the future ports depended on the macroeconomic trends and the strategy was based on expectations for the next 50 years.

In addition to offshore shipping, A.P. Møller – Mærsk provided other services to ensure in-land connectivity and reliable door-to-door transport for its clients. These included multimodal transport (rail, trucking and airfreight), as well as logistics asset-based activities (warehouses, distribution points, inland depots and container freights stations). However, while the significance of these activities for integrating world trade was considerable, the scale of A.P. Møller – Mærsk's investments in inland transport and logistics was still small in comparison to the sums it invested in terminals, vessels and containers. Furthermore, the investments were generally undertaken at times when they would best support the company's global key clients. The extent to which the company undertook these investments varied from country to country based on the cost structure of local operators. In Thailand, for example, A.P. Møller – Mærsk invested in a fully-owned trucking subsidiary that operated as an independent unit, whereas in Vietnam, the company relied on several local subcontractors to ensure reliable door-to-door transportation. In many African countries, A.P. Møller – Mærsk handled most of the inland transportation investments internally and it had, therefore, played a larger role in inland infrastructure development. This could be ascribed to the general lack of local transport service operators as well as the land-locked status of several African countries.

A.P. Møller – Mærsk also eased the global value-chain processes for its MNC clients through its logistic activities, where it played an important role in integrating and coordinating globalised production processes. This was dominantly seen in Maersk Logistics' work and could be identified on several levels. Firstly, by offering services ranging from simple arms-length and standardized, transaction-based services to more complex, tailor-made solution-based services through Maersk Logistics, the company aimed to manage its customers' supply chains more efficiently. This enabled clients from developed and developing countries to manufacture, integrate, and source products and commodities on a global basis. In particular, Maersk Logistics provided supply chain transparency, for which it offered a wide range of e-commerce and information transparency technology services to its customers, services that could be adapted to countries with limited capacity in information technology. As clients received reliable flows of information, market fluctuations were more easily dealt with and potential distortions were prevented.

Secondly, through its extensive local knowledge and market intelligence, A.P. Møller – Mærsk helped its customers reach new markets quicker and with ease. "We are often among the first container shipping companies to enter new markets, which means that we are able to build up a profound knowledge of local markets," an A.P Møller – Mærsk Manager for Southeast Asia said. "When we present our markets to customers, customers request information on the political and economic stability of the country; how secure is the country politically, financially, terrorism wise, and so on".[141] The information it provided ranged from general presentations of markets, including country statistics and economic facts, to more comprehensive market information on business segments, coordination and the business climate.

Thirdly, A.P. Møller – Mærsk brought different firms together. Given its local market knowledge, the company was in a position to identify and recommend reliable, professional, local suppliers to its clients. This was particularly relevant for clients that wished to source in developing countries, where finding and dealing with new suppliers was a process that could prove exceedingly challenging and costly. At the same time, A.P. Møller – Mærsk assisted smaller clients from developing countries who wished to cooperate with suitable global partners. In this respect, Maersk Logistics offered vendor management as part of its supply chain management services.

Mærsk's container business in Vietnam:
Riding the economic wave

> *We have an incredible value in what we do for a country like Vietnam, for development in Vietnam. If Maersk were to withdraw from Vietnam, it would be a big loss for the country. It would mean that larger firms would consider relocating. It would remove large capacity from the market.*
>
> A manager for Maersk Vietnam[142]

A.P. Møller – Mærsk's initial entry into the Vietnamese market came as early as 1991, when it became the first foreign shipping company to enter the country. At the time, Vietnamese law prohibited foreign ownership, so Maersk Sealand (a predecessor to Maersk Line) entered the market by establishing a Vietnamese representative office of Maersk Singapore Pte. Ltd. This market entry was, on the one hand, a response to the company's global key clients, who were increasingly including Vietnam in their sourcing strategies. On the other hand, A.P. Møller – Mærsk's strategic aim was to be at the forefront and to promote new markets for existing and prospective customers. "Mærsk to a large extent follows the interests of their key clients," said a Maersk Vietnam Ltd. manager. "We place investments so that they follow the business of the client. But if we look at the large investments, they are usually placed strategically based on the short and long term estimates of the development of the markets. Here, we almost dictate where demand should occur."[143]

Strategies in emerging markets

Given its early investments in Vietnam, A.P. Møller – Mærsk had taken part in the economic bloom that the country had experienced during the last 15 to 20 years. The average annual GDP growth of 7% to 8% since the early 1990s – figures that made Vietnam the second-fastest growing economy in the world, exceeded only by China – highlighted the fact that the transition from the centralized planned economy to the "socialist market economy" yielded substantial benefits. When the Communist Party's *Đôi mói* ("economic renovation") reforms were introduced at the Sixth Party Congress in 1986, an economic philosophy was initiated that combined government planning with free-trade incentives. Furthermore, it encouraged the establishment of private businesses and foreign investment, including foreign-owned enterprises. This meant that private enterprises and cooperatives played an increasingly significant role in Vietnamese commodity production, while the government maintained control over enterprises considered vital to the national economy. It should, however, be noted that Vietnam's economic growth took off from an extreme low, reflecting the consequences of the Vietnam War (1954 to 1975) and the rather repressive economic measures that were introduced in its aftermath. Therefore, despite the impressive growth figures, poverty and underdevelopment still prevailed to a great extent in Vietnam.

Vietnam increasingly integrated itself with the rest of the world economy. This was evident in its successful entry into various treaties and international organizations: the Association of Southeast Asian Nations (ASEAN) in 1995, the Asia-Pacific Economic Cooperation (APEC) 1998, a Bilateral Trade Agreement with the US in 2000, and the World Trade Organization in January 2007. The WTO membership, in particular, provided an important boost to the country's economy and the continuation of the liberalizing reforms. At the same time, however, the WTO accession created challenges for the economy, as it needed to open up for additional foreign competition. This was particularly relevant for the transportation industry. With greater international exposure, the Vietnamese transport sector increasingly needed to cope with international requirements for integrated transport and communication chains, and services that could ensure reliable, safe transit from seller to buyer. As such, the sector had to match the requirements of multinational corporations. At the same time, low-cost regional competition was expected to arise from China as a result of further liberalization.

In 1993, A.P. Møller – Mærsk successfully acquired the container liner traffic business of the Danish cargo carrier East Asiatic Company, which secured additional access to the Vietnamese transport market. Before it was acquired, East Asiatic Company was engaged in a joint venture with the local agent, Saigon Shipping, where it controlled 75% of the shares. In contrast to many other Vietnamese shipping companies at the time, Saigon Shipping did not belong to

A.P. Møller Mærsk

a governmental ministry in Hanoi. This allowed for more flexibility and eased negotiations. A.P. Møller – Mærsk maintained the 75% share after it acquired East Asiatic Company and it was, therefore, the only carrier with a foreign asset majority in Vietnam. Furthermore, in 1995, Maersk Logistics opened a representative office in Vietnam to provide integrated logistical solutions to its growing Vietnamese customer base.

In 2006, APM Terminals commenced the construction of a deepwater terminal in Cai Mep that would be operative by 2010 with a capacity of approximately 1.1 million TEU per year. Cai Mep International Terminal Co. Ltd. was established as a joint venture between APM Terminals (which controlled 49% of the shares), Saigon Port (one of Vietnam's major port operators, under the administration of the Vietnamese Transport Ministry) and Vietnam National Shipping Lines (a Vietnamese shipping company established in 1997 as part of a governmental reorganization of state-owned enterprises in shipping, ports, stevedoring, ship building and repair, and logistics). The port – covering an area of 48 hectares and with a berth length of 600 meters – would have six high-tech cranes, would include state-of-the-art IT and container handling equipment, and would offer safe, secure and speedy handling of vessels and cargo. As such, the Cai Mep International Terminal would be one the main gateways for exporting and importing cargo in southern Vietnam, which included Ho Chi Minh City, Binh Duong province, Dong Nai province and neighboring provinces.

With this terminal investment, A.P. Møller – Mærsk would be better positioned to meet the growing export and import demand in Vietnam, which was quickly exceeding existing capacity. According to A.P. Møller – Mærsk's regional line manager for southeast Asia, "the scarcity of capacity and lack of depth in Vietnam's ports is clearly a costly element, and ultimately a concern for our customers who import from Vietnam". He further argued that "it is obvious that the big brands, like Nike, Gap and IKEA, not only look at the price and quality of products when they outsource, but also on how the transportation costs will be affected. Growth in Vietnam will, therefore, eventually become more and more dependent on infrastructure improvements".[144]

Creating global opportunities for customers in Vietnam

In conjunction with its goal of ensuring efficient, reliable door-to-door transportation on a global scale, A.P. Møller – Mærsk provided several services for its clients in Vietnam that were related to building physical transport infrastructure as well as integrating and coordinating globalized production processes. With respect to the former, the importance of the company's feeder connectivity for the clients is illustrated through the case of a large, foreign-owned furniture manufacturer in central Vietnam. Prior to partnering up with A.P. Møller – Mærsk, this manufacturer faced relatively high transportation costs, especially in comparison to its competitors in China and Indonesia. This was mainly because the products it manufactured had to be trucked from central Vietnam to Ho Chi Minh City, where they could eventually be transshipped to Singapore and then on to the final destination. When MCC Transport (a feeder subsidiary of A.P. Møller – Mærsk in southeast Asia) started operating feeder ships from central Vietnam to Ho Chi Minh City, however, this client was able to reduce its costs of transport and, consequently, increase its competitiveness. The manager of the foreign-owned furniture manufacturer commented: "Together with Mærsk, we can operate a large business here employing 7,000 people and creating growth for the town and the town port".[145]

As a result of the presence of local operators and contractors with considerable lower cost structures than its own, A.P. Møller – Mærsk had strategically outsourced certain parts of its business model in order to ensure high-quality transportation. As such, Maersk Logistics invested in fully-owned warehousing operations in Vietnam, while it also subcontracted with local and international trucking, rail, airfreight and warehouse operators. The company had, therefore, struck a balance between internalizing and externalizing its activities in Vietnam. This made it easier for MNC clients to use Vietnam as a sourcing country.

The creation of value-chain transparency was a deliberate strategy for A.P. Møller – Mærsk. It was, furthermore, highly relevant, as the poor information technology capacity that characterized the Vietnamese economy complicated business operations, particularly for foreign MNCs. A.P. Møller – Mærsk ensured such transparency by interfacing directly with its clients' systems. This meant that each time a client received an order from a factory in Vietnam, A.P. Møller – Mærsk received the order details as well. This system could cover every detail, from purchase order numbers to stock units and numbers of cartons. The shippers could pull all of this information out of the systems and use it for the booking process. The procedure was thereby made easier for the shippers, and the risk of making mistakes during manual typing was minimized.

Given the centrality of the Vietnamese government in the economy, creating strong and coherent governmental relations was also a deliberate strategy for A.P. Møller – Mærsk. In addition to assisting with obtaining a license to operate, these efforts had played a decisive role in fostering the company's MNC clients in Vietnam. As an A.P. Møller – Mærsk manager in southeast Asia explained: "Take Nike – an important part of their decision to source from Vietnam depends on the government's decision to build deep-sea terminal facilities. Through APM Terminals, we have the financial background and the competences to partner with the Vietnamese government in developing a deep-sea facility. It ties in with our vision to create global opportunities for customers in Vietnam".[146] The decision to construct the new Cai Mep terminal could, therefore, be seen as a means of coping with the general increase in demand for offshore shipping, as well as a means of nurturing the needs and demands of certain key clients.

The customer segments in Vietnam were broadly divided between clients that exported or imported goods to or from the country. The main items exported out of Vietnam, which were handled by A.P. Møller – Mærsk, included furniture, footwear and garments, mainly moving towards Europe and the Pacific. Imported goods, however, were more fragmented, and consisted of foodstuffs, motor vehicles, machinery, timber and metal scrap. These goods generally came from Asia, Europe and the Pacific, although some came from west Africa as well. As such, A.P. Møller – Mærsk's activities in Vietnam mainly served the major trading routes in which the company already held strongholds. In fact, Maersk Line was the market leader in container tonnage capacity on the Europe-Far East and transatlantic trading routes, while it was exceeded by CHKY Alliance and Grand Alliance on the transpacific route (see Exhibit 6). Maersk Line was not, however, strong on inter-Asian trade. This market was highly fragmented, included several discount operators, particularly Chinese, and was subject to low margins.

* * *

Reflecting on the Vietnamese achievements thus far, Thomas Ørting Jørgensen was pleased to see how A.P. Møller – Mærsk's first-mover strategy had paid off. The regional line manager for southeast Asia could, first of all, point to the strong ties the company had with the authorities, which had, among other things, allowed for the granting of operating licenses and contracts in Vietnam. Moreover, the company had succeeded in establishing good relationships with large, important clients undertaking business in the country.

However, Ørting Jørgensen also understood the looming conditions characterizing the economy in Vietnam. Two concerns were at the forefront of his mind. First, he knew that with the booming Vietnamese economy and its continuous liberalization, competition in the transport industry would mount. The privileged position the company had hitherto enjoyed as a result of its early entry could no longer be taken for granted. Of particular concern was the increasing amount of low-cost competition stemming from the neighboring country of China.

Second, A.P. Møller – Mærsk had tied up large amounts of capital in Vietnamese infrastructure, such as the new DKK 1 billion deepwater terminal in Cai Mep. While this bold commitment had put the company ahead of its competitors, it had also increased its exposure, as it meant that it was more dependent on the Vietnamese government than ever before. It was, therefore, a matter of utmost importance to maintain good relations with the government. Moreover,

Strategies in emerging markets

A.P. Møller – Mærsk had bet on continuation of the Vietnamese growth miracle. However, a relatively small country like Vietnam was exceptionally prone to external shocks that could seriously hamper the transportation industry.

Fearing that the advantage arising from A.P. Møller – Mærsk's entrance to Vietnam would eventually evaporate, Ørting Jørgensen felt it was a highly pertinent task to prepare for the altered conditions of tomorrow. However, what to do and how to do it were questions that remained to be answered.

Exhibits for A.P. Møller Mærsk case

Exhibit 1
– The corporate structure of A.P. Møller – Mærsk[147]

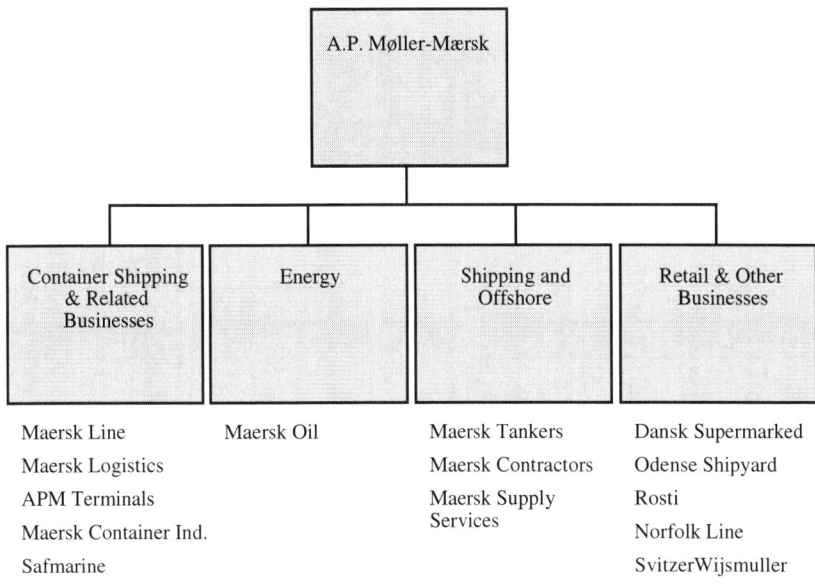

Container Shipping & Related Businesses	Energy	Shipping and Offshore	Retail & Other Businesses
Maersk Line	Maersk Oil	Maersk Tankers	Dansk Supermarked
Maersk Logistics		Maersk Contractors	Odense Shipyard
APM Terminals		Maersk Supply Services	Rosti
Maersk Container Ind.			Norfolk Line
Safmarine			SvitzerWijsmuller

Strategies in emerging markets

Exhibit 2 – A.P. Møller – Mærsk's key figures[148]

Amounts in USD million	2006	2005	2004	2003	2002
Revenue	44,518	34,843	26,490	23,970	19,308
Profit before depreciation, amortization and impairment losses	8,653	8,342	6,735	6,016	4,525
Depreciation, amortization and impairment losses	3,302	2,937	2,118	2,556	2,150
Gains on sale of ships, rigs, etc	711	280	246	99	92
Associated companies – share of profit after tax	484	507	60	61	37
Profit before integration costs	6,546	6,192	4,932	3,620	2,504
Integration costs on acquisition	123	298	-	-	-
Profit before financial items	6,423	5,894	4,923	3,620	2,504
Net financial items	-375	-354	123	229	-87
Value adjustment of financial assets	-	-	832	696	-9
Profit before tax	6,048	5,540	5,878	4,545	2,408
Income tax expenses	3,350	2,218	1,524	1,376	1,038
Profit for the year – continued operations	2,698	3,322	4,354	3,169	1,370
Net result – discontinued operations	25	67	336	-	-
Profit for the year	2,723	3,389	4,690	3,169	1,370
Balance sheet and cash flow					
Total assets	55,409	45,152	33,227	27,491	24,180
Equity	24,148	19,620	18,784	14,042	11,210
Cash flow from operating activities	4,073	5,564	4,849	3,993	3,147
Cash flow from non-current investing activities	5,531	10,467	3,053	2,521	2,299
Investment in property, plant and equipment	7,452	4,815	3,758	2,369	2,083
Key ratios					
Return on equity after tax (%)	12.4	17.6	28.6	25.1	13.5
Equity ratio (%)	43.6	43.5	56.5	51.1	46.4
Earning per share (USD)	636	819	1,135	766	330
Cash flow from operating activities per share (USD)	990	1,352	1,178	970	765
Share price (B-share), end year (USD)	9,397	10,310	8,279	7,117	3,365
Total market capitalization, end year (%)	37,849	41,726	33,903	28,553	13,446
Dividend per share (USD)	97	87	82	50	28

A.P. Møller Mærsk

Exhibit 3 – Financial key figures for the Container Shipping and Related Activities[149]

Amounts in USD million	2006	2005
Revenue	25,275	21,524
Profit before depreciation, amortization and impairment losses	1,544	3,420
Depreciation, amortization and impairment losses	1,611	1,503
Gains on sale of ships, rigs, etc	308	78
Associated companies – share of result after tax	7	18
Profit before integration costs and financial items	248	2,013
Integration costs on acquisition	123	298
Profit before financial items	125	1,715
Net financial items	-392	-191
Profit before tax	-267	1,524
Tax	301	246
Profit for the year	-568	1,278
Balance sheet and cash flow		
Cash flow from operating activities	273	2,500
Cash flow used for investing activities	-2,566	-5,854
Fixed assets	19,163	16,610
Current assets	9,142	7,147
Total assets	28,305	23,757
Non-current liabilities	11,443	9,531
Current liabilities	8,670	4,573
Total liabilities	20,113	14,104

Strategies in emerging markets

Exhibit 4 – The structure of container shipping and related activities[150]

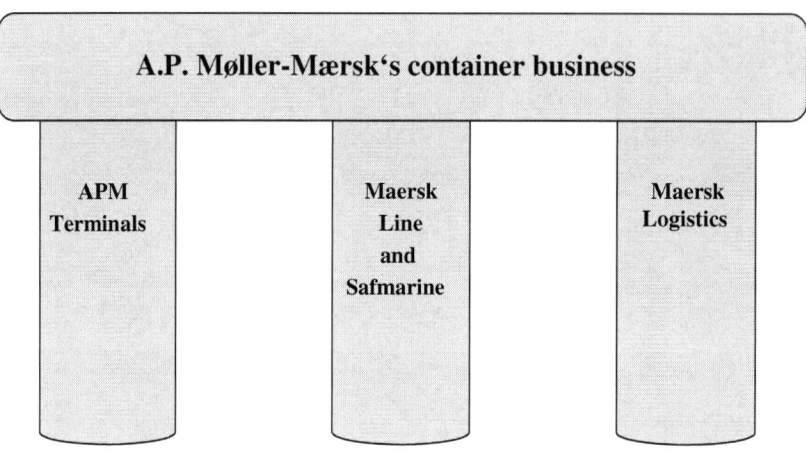

Exhibit 5 – APM Terminals world map[151]

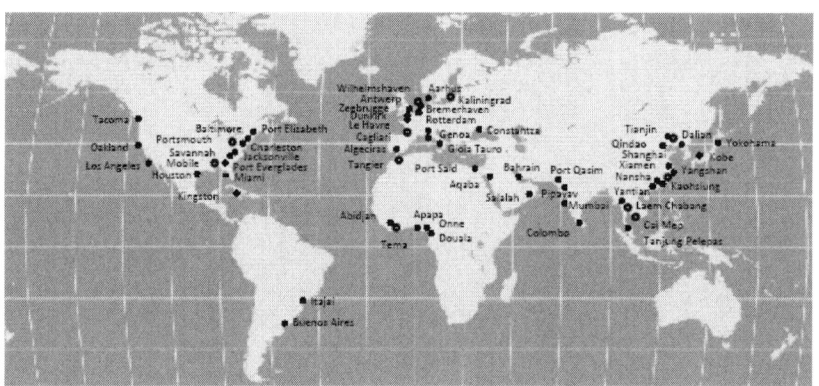

A.P. Møller Mærsk

Exhibit 6 – Global players, market shares[152]

Major players in the container trade, 2006

	Total		% chartered	
Operator[153]	Number	1,000 TEU	1,000 TEU	Avg. ship size in TEU
Maersk-Line	431	1,460.5	53.2	3,389
MSC	229	774.4	36.7	3,382
CMA-CGM	157	468.6	62.2	2,985
Hapaq-Lloyd	127	424.8	43.7	3,345
Evergreen	123	415.4	24.8	3,377
Hanjin	80	329.2	77.2	4,114
Cosco	89	318.1	33.3	3,574
CSCL	70	312.3	49.4	4,461
NYK	99	292.9	49.3	2,959
APL	72	287.7	58.0	3,996
MOL	76	253.3	57.9	3,333
OOCL	54	238.3	37.0	4,412
K-Line	69	231.3	51.3	3,352
Yang-Ming	68	191.8	35.5	2,821
Hamburg-Sud	73	165.1	59.9	2,262
Others/unknown	757	1,595	54.0	2,107
Total	2,574	7,758	49.6	3,014

Global players: tonnage employed by major container trade markets, 2006

	Europe-Far East	Transatlantic	Transpacific
Alliance/operator	1,000 TEU	1,000 TEU	1,000 TEU
Maersk	438.4	183.4	324.9
MSC	229.0	85.1	130.1
CMA-CGM	207.5	14.9	84.1
Evergreen	140.5	50.6	228.6
CHKY Alliance	424.3	18.6	475.8
Grand Alliance	251.3	109.3	330.9
Grand/CP Ships	-	45.6	-
New World Alliance	176.6	52.3	308.5
Total	**1,867.7**	**559.8**	1,882.8

CHAPTER 7

Vestas Wind Systems A/S – Changing winds in the Indian market for wind turbines

The Managing Director of Vestas Wind Technology India Private Ltd, Ramesh Kymal, had been in the Indian wind turbine industry for more than a decade. His journey started at NEG Micon in 1996, which merged with the vast and rapidly expanding Vestas India operation in 2003. By 2008, Vestas' Indian adventure had developed into two large assembly sites: one in Chennai, which produced hubs and nacelles for the export market, and another in Pondicherry, which produced for the domestic Indian market. By 2008, the Indian market was the fifth largest in the world and had potential capacity of producing 45,000 MW, valued at USD 94 billion. Kymal was especially pleased to see that the Indian operation had been given Vestas's global mandate of producing the V82-1.65 MW turbine: "Having India as part of Vestas global manufacturing capacity for the V82-1.65 MW turbine is an acknowledgement of our Indian set-up and is based on India's advantages of know-how, infrastructure, strength in manufacturing and the ongoing focus to enhance competitiveness".[154]

However, recent success stories could not hide the fact that Vestas, after decades of Indian maneuvering, had failed to confidently consolidate its position. Sales figures were waning and there were still problems of ensuring that Indian suppliers would deliver according to Vestas's standards. The merger between NEG Micon and Vestas in 2003 had consumed enormous resources, and still created coordination difficulties given the two companies' different technologies and supply chains. Moreover, Indian newcomers were muscling their way into the wind turbine market, leaving Vestas with a mediocre market share. Kymal knew that all of these problems could, to some degree, be attributed to the long, troubled history of Vestas India and that only a thorough analysis of the experiences of the past would allow him to solve the challenges of the present and the future.

Strategies in emerging markets

Introducing Vestas Wind Systems A/S

Vestas Wind Systems A/S manufactured and installed wind turbines (see Exhibit 1) delivering electricity at competitive prices. Under the overarching corporate strategy of becoming "No. 1 in Modern Energy", the company strived to position itself as the market leader at the same time as it was promoting the industry as a whole to place wind energy on par with oil and gas. The "No. 1 in Modern Energy" strategy had replaced "The Will to Win 2005-2008" strategy, which had transformed the company from its status as a mere Danish producer of wind power turbines into a global energy and technology company. With the broad, worldwide awareness of global climatic changes, the economic as well as political eagerness to choose wind power as a preferred energy source had strengthened over years. Moreover, modern wind turbines were developed to such an extent that they were becoming increasingly competitive with conventional energy sources.

Vestas was headed by an Executive Committee under CEO Ditlev Engel. The company consisted of 15 business units with clear division of responsibilities within sales, production and development. "Vestas Excellence" was a cross-organizational unit that aimed to increase quality, productivity and profitability, and to avoid and eliminate "silo" thinking in the respective business units. The company also had a Customer Advisory Board, which focused on customer relations, and a Vestas Technology R&D unit, which emphasized innovation and development (see Exhibit 2).

Products, technology and competitors
One salient feature about Vestas was that it produced its blades, towers and control systems in-house. This vertical integration approach, which was in contrast to most of its competitors, gave Vestas a number of advantages. As former CEO Johannes Poulsen noted, "we produce more in-house than most others in the industry. That gives us the necessary know-how and we can keep an eye on quality at all times. When something is about to go wrong, we are faster and better at finding solutions because we do not have to start a discussion with the supplier about whose fault it is". He added that "on the other hand, we must admit that if a dramatic turn occurs in the market, then we have larger capacity costs than others do".[155] The main exception to this rule of internalization was the production of the important gearboxes, which was outsourced to close, well-nurtured suppliers. This was somewhat of a paradox, as the gearbox was considered to be of Vestas's absolute competitive strengths.

In terms of product development, Vestas had improved the efficiency of turbines dramatically over the course of 30 years. The reliability of the mills had improved significantly, which led to fewer windmill deficiencies and less downtime. As such, the windmills were expected to operate for 20 years without the need to change anything but oil and grease. This high reliability was essential for Vestas, as the company, through contractual warranties on its windmills, incurred losses if the mills did not perform as promised.

In the 2000s, Vestas became the world's largest wind turbine producer. It displayed sensational growth rates, doubled its workforce between 2004 and 2008, and increased its revenues almost three-fold (see Exhibit 3). However, Vestas was not the only company fighting for shares in the lucrative wind energy market, and it faced increasingly competent international competitors. Among these were Siemens Wind Power of Germany, Gamesa of Spain, GE Wind of the US, Sinovel and Goldwin of China, and Suzlon of India. As competition intensified, Vestas's overall market share fell from 23% in 2007 to 19.8% in 2008 despite the 25% annual growth in the global market.

Internationalization pattern and strategy
Vestas had mainly followed a strategy of organic growth. Internationalization had been gradual and Denmark was the undisputed basis for servicing world markets. The strategy was focused on a relatively narrow range of key markets. After experiencing strong growth in the first half of the 1980s, Vestas faced a severe crisis with huge deficits in the mid 1980s. The industry almost collapsed when the US state subsidies were cut back and Vestas faced mounting difficulties.

To manage this predicament, Vestas initiated a comprehensive restructuring process in 1986-87, during which it divested large parts of the group. The new Vestas – with a new CEO, Johannes Poulsen, and with a Dutch investment fund as majority owner – embarked on a more diversified internationalization strategy with sales spread across a growing number of markets. Looking back, Vestas largely attributed the crisis to its rather narrow focus on the US and the Danish markets. The new markets included India, China, Australia, North and South America, and Europe. By the mid 1990s, the company exported 9 out of 10 produced windmills and was active in 30 countries.

One market in which Vestas was actively engaged was Spain. In 1999, Spain was Vestas's largest market and it also owned a large stake in Gamesa E'elica S.A. – a joint venture with a local Spanish partner. The Spanish market was lucrative given its many suitable locations for windmills and the general interest from Spanish investors. In 2001, Vestas divested itself from its 40% share in Gamesa. This was a decision that would later come back to haunt the company – by 2008, Gamesa had become one of Vestas's largest competitors, partly building its offering on the basis of Vestas technology.

Throughout the 1990s, the two Danish wind turbine producers NEG Micon and Vestas were constantly bidding against each other for the position as the world's leading windmill producer, and both were continuously expanding into

Strategies in emerging markets

new markets. Like Vestas, NEG Micon had abandoned its narrow internationalization strategy of the 1980s and early 1990s. As NEG Micon CEO Torben Bjerre-Madsen pointed out after the very difficult year of 1999, "we shall not again become dependent on individual markets, as we were in the US. Our efforts must be spread to more large markets and fewer small ones, so that growth can be controlled. Germany, Spain, Denmark are the main markets, but the US will also see a share of our sales as the country is opening up to supporting mills again".[156] India, China and Japan were also viewed as important potential markets for NEG Micon. The two companies were, therefore, challenging each other in an ever-increasing number of markets.

This rivalry disappeared in 2003, however, when the two companies merged into Vestas Wind Systems A/S. The merger was, among other things, motivated by changes in market conditions, where an increasing amount of revenue and sales came from established power utility companies buying large windmill parks and offshore projects, both of which required greater capacity and higher expenditures. As a consolidated business, the two companies accounted for about 36% of the windmill capacity delivered globally in 2003.

In 2005, Ditlev Engel was appointed CEO of Vestas. Engel faced a number of huge challenges. The merger between NEG Micron and Vestas had failed to yield the intended financial results and was hampering growth. Moreover, the company possessed a business setup that was losing its competitiveness: while Vestas was competing for markets around the world, the clear majority of its production sites were in Europe (mainly Denmark). Not only did this entail high labor, overhead and transportation costs, but it also caused problems in terms of landing bigger contracts, as such contracts were often dependent local presence and production. With Engel as CEO, Vestas embarked upon a cost-reducing and market-seeking strategy to optimize the entire business system. One example of this strategy was Vestas's 2005 decision to transfer a number of assembly jobs from Denmark to Spain. In this way, Vestas could be closer to the large Spanish and southern European markets, while it could also save on labor and transportation. In 2005, the production internationalization strategy accelerated and, by 2009, Vestas had production facilities in Europe, Australia, India, China and the US.

Vestas Wind Systems India Pvt. Ltd.

Vestas's Indian arrival
Although Vestas had been present in India as early as the mid 1980s, when it attempted to find feasible investments partners, and convince politicians of the advantages and possibilities associated with windmills, it took a large grant by the Danish aid agency DANIDA to India to motivate Vestas's formal entry into the

Indian market. The DANIDA grant funded an Indian windmill project valued at DKK 185 million, and it was intended to kick-start India's production of wind energy. The money was granted on the condition that the windmills be bought in Denmark. Consequently, Vestas and NEG Micon each delivered and installed 10 MW, distributed over three windmill parks in Tamil Nadu and Gujarat.

In order to successfully establish themselves on the Indian market, however, it was necessary for Vestas and NEG Micon to consider how to enter and operate in the market. At the time, foreign direct investment in India was covered by a number of stringent, regulatory requirements imposed by the Indian government. For instance, the government placed an 85% tax on imported towers and a 25% tax on imported blades (as blades were not produced in India at the time). Moreover, the Indian government mandated Indian co-ownership of operations, and it only allowed FDI in certain activities.

In continuation of the DANIDA project, NEG Micon entered into a production and sales licensing agreement with the Indian firm NEPC in 1992. NEG Micon held only a tiny share of NEPC, and the collaboration consisted primarily of the licensing agreement, some knowledge transfer and sales of components. NEPC did not use the NEG Micon brand on the mills it installed, and while NEG Micon's licensing agreement paved the way into the Indian market for its windmills, the agreement meant that NEG Micon could only be present in India through NEPC. In addition, production and assembly were undertaken solely by NEPC, without NEG Micon having any control over the production process or the technology used. Despite the fact that an estimated 85% of the production of NEG Micon windmills was carried out in India, technologically key components, such as electronic steering systems and blades, had to be imported. The joint venture was successful in terms of market share; by March 1992, when NEG Micon's windmill number 100 was set up by NEPC, the company represented half of the installed wind energy capacity in India. However, quality problems, overselling and ineffective after-sales services jeopardized the reputation of the industry. When the Indian government softened the requirements for local ownership in 1996, NEG Micon immediately set up a fully-owned subsidiary, which was later to become the backbone of Vestas's Indian operation.

Vestas settled for a joint-venture agreement with the local RRB Energy in 1992, which was named Vestas RRB. Vestas owned 49% of the joint venture, which gave the company considerably more leverage over the production and sales processes than NEG Micon had. Consequently, Vestas invested large amounts of time and money in training the Indian employees involved in the joint venture. The long-term ambition was to produce entire windmills in India, as production costs were lower in India and because Vestas strove to make India its Asian spearhead. Nevertheless, two years after the joint venture was established, only about 40% of the windmills were locally produced and the blades

Strategies in emerging markets

were still manufactured in Denmark – a result of quality concerns and Vestas Denmark's desire to protect key propriety knowledge.

Building an Indian mandate

The 2003 merger of Vestas and NEG Micon meant that Vestas suddenly possessed two companies in India: Vestas RRB and NEG Micon (India) Pvt. Ltd. Initially, Ditlev Engel indicated that he had no intention to change this setup.[157] However, in 2006, the 49% share in Vestas RRB was divested and the NEG Micon activities were renamed Vestas Wind Technology India Pvt. Ltd. The change in name was part of the strategic repositioning of Vestas's operations in India, as the Danish management increasingly recognized the untapped capacity of the Indian workforce and the vast potential of the domestic market.

By 2008, the Indian market was the Vestas's ninth-largest market in terms of delivered MW, and the fourth largest in terms of the number of windmills delivered. Commenting on the promising Indian market, the Managing Director of Vestas Wind Technology India, Ramesh Kymal, stated: "It's like IT and India – ten years ago, no one knew the potential India had. Today, India is a leader in IT. The situation is the same with wind energy. At the moment, people are unaware of our capacity, but the fact is we have a very strong technical workforce and intellectual capacity here that is relatively cheap. And this expertise is available not just for India, but for the rest of the world as well. In terms of our domestic situation, the potential is also great. India is in desperate need of new sources of affordable energy to maintain its high economic growth – and we have the expertise needed to meet this challenge."[158]

Some observers warned that selling the 49% share in Vestas RRB meant risking that a local competitor, similar to Gamesa, could be created. However, Torben N. Rasmussen, Managing Director of Vestas Asia Pacific, viewed the transaction as a necessary strategic move: "We are selling to create the necessary focus. Vestas RRB has its focus on small mills, while in Vestas we generally have a focus on selling medium and larger mills. In that regard, we have evaluated that, even though we still collaborate on the technical side, it is best that we invest where we can see our future strategy, that is, in medium and larger mills."[159]

The mandate to produce the 750 kW and the V82-1.65 MW windmills was originally intended for the domestic Indian market. According to Kymal, the V82-1.65 MW was the ideal turbine size for India for several reasons: "The V82 is good for a low-to-medium wind region like India and it is very price competitive. It is also ideal because the roads in India cannot handle bigger turbines. But in the future, as the larger turbines become lighter, we may also be able to use them."[160] However, it soon became evident that this windmill could also achieve successful sales in the Asia Pacific region, and India started servicing regional markets as well. Therefore, after the strategic change, Vestas India appeared to be positioning itself to become a more important part of the global manufacturing setup. Apart from the enhanced production mandate, there were signs that the Vestas India would be assigned greater responsibilities for specific value-chain functions. For instance, in 2007, Vestas Technology R&D Chennai Pvt. Ltd. was established as a wholly owned Vestas subsidiary, functioning as part of the global R&D efforts, but it did not evolve from Vestas India. Vestas Technology R&D Chennai was designed as an R&D back office, which was meant to source mechanical and IT engineers.[161] The office expanded its activities and provided, for example, product support R&D for the wind turbine model that was only produced in India. The workforce increased to around 130 by the end of 2008, or 20% of the total R&D staff of Vestas Wind Systems.

Building an Indian sourcing platform
Roughly half of the total value of windmills assembled by Vestas Wind Technology India Pvt. Ltd. was imported, mainly from Europe. Imports typically included high-tech components, such as generators, bearings, control panels and brake systems. There were several reasons for importing these components, including proprietary concerns, the wish to protect Vestas's know-how and a lack of sufficiently capable local suppliers. In addition, the process of developing suppliers with sufficient skills was expensive and time demanding. Vestas India was therefore constantly identifying potential local suppliers whose capabilities could, if certain investments were made, meet Vestas's high requirements and standards. Given the initial lack of competent local suppliers, however, Vestas actively encouraged its European, and especially Danish, suppliers to follow it into the Indian market. As a result, a cluster of Danish wind turbine suppliers eventually materialized in southern India around Bangalore and Chennai. Among these companies were AVN Hydraulic, Hydra Grene and Steel Cluster.

The Danish producer of blades, LM Glasfiber, also followed the Danish wind-turbine producers to India. It was established in Denmark as a furniture producer before it expanded into sailboats, and eventually, in 1978, into blades. By 2008, it had production facilities in Denmark, Spain, Holland, Germany, the US, India and China, and was the world's leading supplier of blades. Vestas, however, was not just another customer for LM Glasfiber. Blade production was considered to be one of Vestas's core competencies and was normally kept in-house. Indeed, LM Glasfiber only delivered blades to Vestas in India – a collaborative arrangement that was a remnant from the time when NEG Micon was a competitor to Vestas and LM Glasfiber had been a supplier of blades to NEG Micon. Reflecting on the somewhat atypical collaboration, Søren Knudsen, Sales and Marketing Director of LM Glasfiber, noted that "This is the first agreement we have made with the new Vestas and it is something we are very happy about,

Strategies in emerging markets

as Vestas is the largest windmill manufacturer in the world". He further said that "this is a three-year agreement for a considerable market for both of us and we do have to get going first, but it is naturally our hope that the collaboration can be expanded. We have a lot of good suggestions for new markets that we are discussing with Vestas". Correspondingly, Vestas's Communications Officer, Peter Kruse, explained that "production of blades is a core area for Vestas, and the agreement in India is a continuation of something old. We still keep blade production close to the heart". The sourcing agreement between the two companies was extended by three years in 2006 to run until the end of 2009.[162]

Indian government policies
The Indian market for windmills was driven by the demand for a secure energy supply, and in this respect, the Indian government offered a number of favorable subsidy schemes (See Exhibit 4). As such, two key factors were particularly conducive for growth in India. First, windmill owners were allowed to completely write off the windmill in the first year after its acquisition and the respective company was given a five-year tax break. Second, power supplies were very unstable in India, with power often being cut off for up to several hours per day. Many industrial companies were, therefore, interested in buying windmills in order to secure a stable supply of electricity.

Although the forecasts for the Indian windmill industry looked optimistic in the mid 1990s, the situation was negatively affected by developments in 1996 and 1997. Following the Indian parliament elections in 1996 and the victory of the Hindu traditionalist party BJP, a general economic slowdown ensued with the adoption of new duties, and bureaucratic delays in land conferral and environmental approvals. As a consequence of defaulting customers and the lack of payment guarantees, Vestas suffered losses of DKK 185 million in 1997. Moreover, in 1998, many of the installed Danish windmills in India were literally toppled by strong cyclones. This was in contrast to, for instance, mills erected by German Enercon, which were based on a stronger construction. However, contrary to many of their competitors, Vestas and Micon managed to remain active in the market and strengthened their positions when the market picked up in the following years. In 1999, Vestas landed an order to install 30 windmills in Tamul Nadu in another project sponsored by DANIDA. In the same year, the Indian government provided a new boost to the market by proposing reforms that would remove taxes on renewable energy, grant automatic approval of windmills of up to 5MW, offer cheaper loans and establish a state-driven electricity company that would invest in larger windmill projects.

The rise of Indian competitors
The Indian company Suzlon Energy Ltd. was India's largest windmill producer

and a major competitor to Vestas. In 2004, Suzlon was indisputably the market leader in India with a 43% market share. Vestas was second with a 32% share.[163] In 2007, Suzlon increased its share to 59.6% of the total MW installed in India, while Vestas only installed 8.8% (see Exhibit 5). Suzlon was not only challenging Vestas in the Indian market, but it was also rapidly becoming a global rival. From having virtually no internal activities in 2000, Suzlon had become a major challenger to the industry incumbents by the late 2000s. In 2007, it controlled a global market share of more than 10% compared to Vestas's 23%.

As an expression of the increasingly global nature of the rivalry between Vestas and Suzlon, the Indian company established a subsidiary in Vestas's home market, Denmark, in 2004. The subsidiary functioned as the company's international headquarters and as a holding company for all of its activities outside India. In 2006, Suzlon acquired Belgium's Hansen, a gear box producer holding 25% of the world market for gear boxes and a major supplier for Vestas. Through the acquisition of German REpower in 2007, Suzlon further consolidated its position by adding capabilities to produce the largest mills in its portfolio. The Managing Director of Suzlon Energy A/S in Denmark was Per Hornung Pedersen, who acted as CFO in NEG Micon prior to coming to Suzlon. With labor costs constituting just 3% of total turnover due to the full Indian production, compared to 16% for Vestas, Suzlon had the potential to become a major global player and, therefore, a challenger for Vestas. Pedersen pointed out that "one-third of all windmills standing in India are from Suzlon and quality is also an issue India. You cannot operate at this level if you cannot produce the same quality as others can deliver. Previously, that has not been an issue for the customers".[164]

Another local competitor was Vestas RRB, the result of Vestas's joint venture with RRB Energy. Although it operated in a different segment than Vestas Wind Systems, RRB invested about DKK 139 million in 2005 in setting up a blades factory with a capacity to produce 700 blades a year. RBB's managing director estimated that producing blades in India, rather than importing them, would lower the price by 10% to 15% and reduce delivery time from 120 days to a mere 40 days.[165] Moreover, in 2006, RRB entered into an agreement with Dutch Windbrokers to sell windmills in Europe, North America and South America. While it might appear that Vestas had nurtured a future competitor, just as it had done with Gamesa in Spain, Vestas Wind Systems did not see the ambitions of RRB as a problem yet, as the RRB mills were smaller and, as such, did not conflict with Vestas' product line.

* * *

Ramesh Kymal reflected over the achievements of Vestas in India over the past decade. Two distinct companies and former arch rivals – Vestas and NEG Micon – had been integrated, albeit with great difficulties. Huge investments in identifying and developing local Indian suppliers had paid off, and Vestas India was positioned to produce turbines using cheap Indian inputs that could still meet Vestas's standards. Vestas India had obtained a global product mandate for certain turbines and positioned itself as a possible global sourcing platform for components and services in a situation where Vestas's headquarters was contemplating dismissals of high-salary European workers due to cost pressures. Even advanced R&D activities were being located in India.

The question for Kymal was whether he could seize this window of opportunity to consolidate and advance India's mandate within the group. Would he be able to circumvent the reputation stemming from Vestas's long and troubled entry into India, which still permeated parts of the organization? Would he be able to obtain the mandate that he believed India was capable of fulfilling? Kymal knew that the future challenges of promoting India within an essentially Danish company would be no less daunting than they had been during the building of a viable operation in India.

Exhibits for Vestas Wind Systems A/S case

Vestas Wind Systems A/S

Exhibit 1 – Wind turbine technical specifications[166]

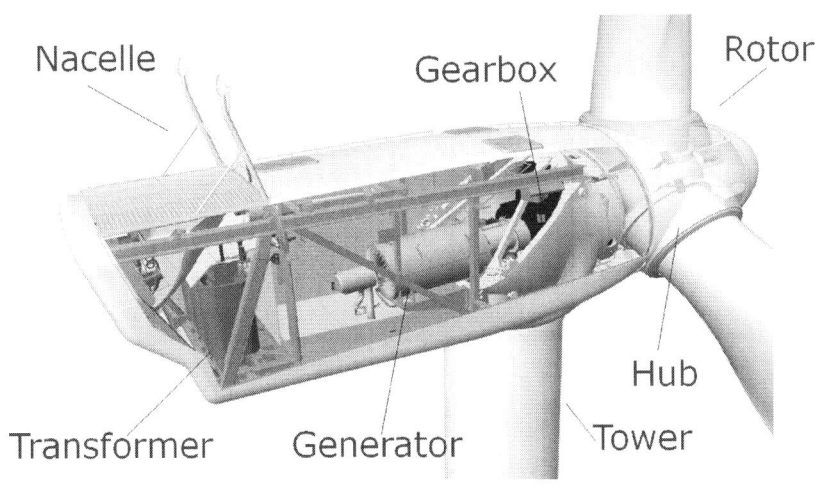

Exhibit 2 – Corporate structure[167]

Vestas Wind Systems A/S	
	Corporate functions
Vestas Nacelles	Vestas Asia Pacific
Vestas Blades	Vestas Central Europe
Vestas Towers	Vestas Northern Europe
Vestas Control Systems	Vestas Americas
Vestas Spare Parts	Vestas Mediterranean
Vestas Technology R&D	Vestas China
Vestas People & Culture	Vestas Offshore

151

Strategies in emerging markets

Exhibit 3 – Vestas's key figures[168]

Amounts in EURm	2008	2007	2006	2005	2004
Revenue	6,035	4,861	3,854	3,583	2,363
Gross profit	1,179	825	461	84	120
Operating profit/(loss) (EBIT)	668	443	201	-116	-49
Profit/(loss) for the year	511	291	111	-192	-61
Employees					
Nr of employees at the end of the year	20,829	15,305	12,309	10,618	9,594

Exhibit 4
– Existing wind power incentives in India by the mid 2000s[169]

Accelerated depreciation of up to 80% of the total project cost, resulting in income tax saving in any existing business.

Income generated from the sale of wind power is tax-free for a block of 10 consecutive years for 15 years from the commissioning date.

Wheeling of power: The power generated by the wind farm can be wheeled to the consumption point of any developer through the government-owned grid at a nominal wheeling charge of 5% to 10%.

Banking: The excess power generated in a particular month can be banked for utilization later during the year for a nominal charge.

Power purchase: The power generated by the windfarms shall be sold to the state utility at prices varying from USD 0.05 to USD 0.07 (varies from state to state).

Power purchase agreements (10-20 years) are signed by the utilities in most states of the country.

Exhibit 5 – Market shares in India, 2007[170]

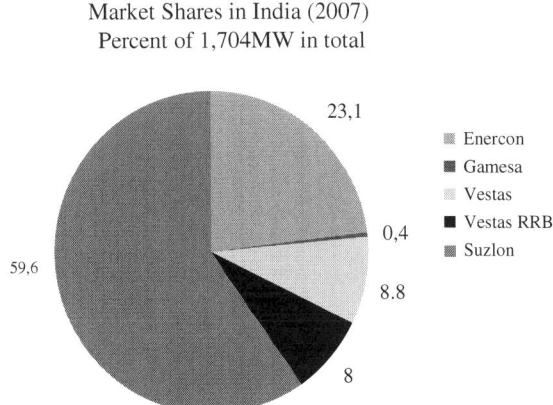

CHAPTER 8

Danfoss in China
– Taking on the kingdom in the middle

By 2009, Danfoss China was facing the challenge of entering and gaining market shares in the large and expanding Chinese mid-segment markets for adapted versions of the group's different product ranges. Following many years of doing business in China, Danfoss had gained important footholds in the country. The company had a strong management team in place, consisting mainly of local people possessing important knowledge of Chinese conditions. It had, moreover, set up a number of large, well-functioning manufacturing facilities, and it nurtured good, active relations with the Chinese authorities. Furthermore, it had a market-leading position as the preferred supplier to a number of global buyers within air-conditioning and refrigeration.

As the Chinese economy was on the rise, the domestic Chinese market was following suit, growing at an unparalleled speed. However, Danfoss was missing out on the large Chinese mid-segment market. Given its huge growth potential and its likely future strategic importance, Danfoss was considering carving out a stronghold as imperative. There was a real danger that local Chinese competitors would be given room to develop and upgrade their own products within this segment. This could eventually result in a situation in which Danfoss's market shares for high-segment products would slowly be eaten up from below. Moreover, if Danfoss was beaten in China, the upcoming Chinese competitors could challenge Danfoss in the global market.

However, while the Danfoss management recognized the danger coming from Chinese challenger firms, it was also aware that the company could not risk undermining its brand name in pursuing the Chinese mid segment. Danfoss's products had traditionally been sold at premium prices on the basis of the company's reputation for high quality and reliable delivery and this strategy had, after all, helped sustain profits for many years (see Exhibit 1). It was, therefore, not a trivial challenge regarding market strategy that Danfoss faced in China.

Strategies in emerging markets

Introducing the Danfoss Group
As one of the largest Danish companies, the manufacturing group Danfoss strived to be a "global leader within our core businesses, as a highly respected company, which improves quality of life by mastering advanced technologies in customer applications while creating value for all stakeholders".[171]

Danfoss was founded in 1933 as a producer of valves for refrigerators. The company started gaining continental European market shares during World War II as a result of the mainland's isolation from the UK and the US. Subsequently, Danfoss increased its geographic scope and product range as its original product markets reached saturation. With the rising energy prices of the 1970s, the company experienced significant growth, especially in its production of radiator thermostats (a product facilitating reduced energy consumption). The 1980s was a period characterized by the improvement of existing products, the introduction of new products to existing customers, and the development of complete systems that integrated electronics and precision machines.

Danfoss became a well-established brand by maintaining a high-quality standard in production and products, ensuring accurate deliveries and developing customer relations. The company operated with the slogan of "Making modern living possible", and its core values centered on ensuring trust, representing a safe and reliable choice, being passionate about technology, having a global culture with local representation, and being environmentally and socially responsible.

The organization of Danfoss
The Danfoss organization was based on its three main product divisions: Refrigeration & Air Conditioning (RA), Heating (HE) and Motion Controls (MC). In addition, Danfoss acquired majority ownership in Sauer-Danfoss in 2007 – one of the world's leading manufacturers and suppliers of mobile hydraulics and related equipment for off-road vehicles. Moreover, an underlying Services Division (SE) was responsible for internal services, logistics and IT (see Exhibit 2). RA was the largest of the three product divisions with annual turnover of DKK 11.2 billion in 2007. The HE division accounted for DKK 6.2 billion in turnover, while MC accounted for DKK 4.4 billion. Sauer-Danfoss's net sales were approximately DKK 10 billion. Each product division was organized as an independent business unit that reported directly to Danfoss's top management, and each unit held overall responsibility for its specific products. This meant that each division undertook production and procurement of its line of products, as well as R&D, marketing and sales. The organization was further supported by Danfoss Ventures, which was responsible for developing and promoting new business ventures across all divisions.

Danfoss's Executive Committee was headed by CEO Niels B. Christiansen, who had been a member of the Executive Committee for four years prior to becoming CEO in late 2008. The Board of Directors was headed by former CEO and member of the owning family, Jørgen Mads Clausen.

One central, overarching concept spanning the entire Danfoss group and its different divisions was the Danfoss Business System (DBS). DBS consisted of four cross-divisional programs in production, purchasing, sales and product development. The programs were designed to equip the different parts of the group and their employees with a common set of tools that would enable them to enhance their performance, save costs on raw materials and components, increase sales and identify new sales areas, and improve the understanding of the customers' needs. As such, the business system could be seen as an attempt to impose lean principles in Danfoss, and the company aimed to have DBS fully integrated with the entire organization in 2013.[172]

Global culture
Danfoss's global HR organization aimed to create a culture that "drives performance improvements and Will to Win and that is fully in line with the Core Values".[173] In this respect, being "local everywhere"[174] – having a global culture with a local representation – was emphasized. Additionally, it was CEO Christiansen's ambition to "work even closer with the customers",[175] just as he advocated a management philosophy of delegating responsibilities to people with local knowledge and competencies. He therefore stressed that top management must be mobile and ready to travel in order to meet local management and customers in their home locations.

99% of Danfoss was owned by the founding family and its foundation, the Mads and Bitten Clausen Foundation. There had been rumors of an initial public offering, but these were dispelled by the newly appointed CEO in 2008. Christiansen maintained that the group had sufficient capital and market positions necessary to continue under family ownership.[176] Exempt from this ownership structure, however, was Sauer-Danfoss, in which Danfoss had a 55.4% controlling share.

The dividend rate was increased to 25% in 2008 from 20% in 2007. There was also a marked increase in the group's debt to equity ratio from 38% in 2007 to 82% in 2008. To a large extent, this could be explained by the acquisition of the shareholder majority in Sauer-Danfoss as well as the continuously increasing investments in China. In fact, the latter increased by 122% from 2007 to 2008.

International orientation
Danfoss's goal, as stated by Jørgen Mads Clausen when he took on the position as CEO in 1996, was to be number one or two globally in all its product ranges

Strategies in emerging markets

(see Exhibit 3). Danfoss owned 70 factories in about 25 countries and had a daily production capacity of 250,000 units. The RA division alone had 36 factories in 14 countries. Although Danfoss produced a wide range of products, Clausen denied that the company was a conglomerate, insisting that Danfoss "would have been [a conglomerate] if we owned a number of firms that, on the face of it, were not connected. But all our divisions are closely related".[177] By 2008, he concluded that the goal had been achieved for 80% of the products.[178] When Clausen resigned from the post as CEO that year, he announced that Danfoss was ready to grow three-fold over the next 12 years, implying a turnover of DKK 100 billion and a workforce of 100,000 employees by 2020.[179]

On the group level, Europe had always been the market accounting for the highest turnover, with Germany being the country with the highest sales. The US market was Danfoss's second-largest market in terms of sales, although this market did not achieve net profit until 2005. China was considered to be Danfoss's second home market, where the target was to reach market shares similar to those in Europe. It had grown from being the eighth-largest market in 2006 to the fourth largest in 2007. Russia became the group's third-largest market in 2008, with the heating division accounting for 60% of sales. In relation to emerging markets, CEO Christiansen expected China, Russia and India to together account for 25% of Danfoss's total sales by 2011.[180]

Danfoss had altered its internationalization and growth strategies several times. Originally, growth was achieved organically. Danfoss often entered new geographical markets through sales and, subsequently, production of radiator thermostats, as the thermostat was a product that quickly reached a sales volume that was sufficient for profitable production. However, after the 1980s, growth through acquisitions was favored. The general acquisition strategy had been to strengthen market positions by finding companies whose products complemented Danfoss's product range – products that could be marketed through its existing distribution network. However, after the acquisition of the majority post in Sauer-Danfoss in 2008, Danfoss would, according to CFO Frederik Lotz, probably return to its organic growth strategy.[181]

Danfoss in China: discovering the mid-end market

Initially, China was just one of many markets for Danfoss, where it slowly expanded production to take advantage of the low Chinese wages. Some of the output was exported and sold worldwide, and some was sold to large Chinese producers and multinational OEMs. As business picked up and Chinese turnover soared from DKK 275 million in 2001 to DKK 1.14 billion in 2007, the company increasingly focused on positioning itself as a leader within the premium high-end segments of its various product ranges. Danfoss had expanded its original entry strategy based on radiator thermostats to encompass other activities, such as servicing producers of refrigerators and air conditioners. Danfoss had, therefore, been able to increase its overall production and sales in China exponentially since the company first started out in China and had opened a large number of subsidiaries in China (see Exhibit 4). Danfoss China had become the second-biggest place of employment in the group with staff numbering almost 3,000 in its five local factories and eight sales offices by the end of 2008 (see Exhibit 5).

The Chinese organization

In many ways, Danfoss China was an exact replica of Danfoss's global organization with three product divisions. Danfoss China had three division heads, each reporting to the Danfoss China CEO. However, they also reported to the global division heads and, in case of disagreements, the global heads had the final word. The CEO of Danfoss China reported to the COO of the Executive Committee. Each division in China had all of the functions and units that the global divisions had, including an operations unit, a sales unit and an R&D unit. Likewise, corporate functions, such as finance, HR and legal support, as well as a Danfoss Business System China unit, were used as support functions in Danfoss China.

The Chinese subsidiary was headed by the head of the Chinese RA division, which was the largest division in China by far. It had ownership of what could be compared to a production park, in which other Danfoss units could lease production areas and facilities, as well as corporate support functions when needed. Excess expenditures on constructing manufacturing facilities in the early stages of entry were thereby avoided, and the other facilities were able to investigate the possibilities in the Chinese market before deciding whether to undertake more extensive investments.

An essential task was to achieve a balance between Chinese and Danish management. One articulated goal was that the management of Danfoss China should be "localized" and not filled with expatriates. Management positions that had previously been occupied by expatriates and became vacant were filled with Chinese employees. Indeed, it was a long-term intention to eventually create a fully local Chinese management without any expatriates.

The Chinese entry strategy

Danfoss had been selling products on a small scale to the Chinese market through agents in Hong Kong since the 1960s. In 1994, Danfoss opened its own sales offices in Hong Kong. These sales offices faced heavy taxes and other restrictions when exporting to China, but their establishment was necessary if Danfoss was to enter the Chinese market, as Chinese regulations at the time required that foreign enterprises should have local production in order to set up sales offices in mainland China. In 1993, Danfoss was granted a business license to open a

Strategies in emerging markets

wholly owned subsidiary in China. When production commenced in China in the mid-1990s, the company used rented factory space but its first factory was ready by 1997. Clausen believed that it was to Danfoss's advantage to be able to start as a wholly owned subsidiary instead of a joint venture, as many joint ventures had proven difficult for Western companies doing business in China.[182]

Initially, the establishment of facilities for the production of radiator thermostats in Wuqing, near Beijing, did not appear to be successful. The investment in Wuqing had very much been in line with Danfoss's traditional investment strategy. Having learned from previous challenges at setting up production in Mexico, where too many changes were undertaken over too short a period of time, initial production in Wuqing stuck to well known processes. The strategy of focusing on radiator thermostats was made in anticipation of Chinese government policies aimed at reducing the energy consumption used for heating by 50% by 2002. However, although the conditions for success had been laid, the market for Danfoss's radiator thermometers never took off. Although Danfoss allegedly failed to close the negotiations on delivering thermostats to a planned residential district with 200,000 inhabitants as a result of the Danish government's criticism of the human rights conditions in China,[183] the market was inherently difficult, as Chinese energy prices were not fixed according to consumption but according to the ground area of people's homes.

Eventually however, and in large part due to a seemingly unexpected success as a supplier to the major producers of cooling and air-conditioning systems in southern China, Danfoss's Chinese adventure paid off. Thus, Danfoss shifted its focus to the production and sales of compressors for refrigerators in China, catering to exporting multinational producers of air-conditioning units and refrigerators. These multinational clients were mainly located in southern China, where Danfoss started the construction of a new factory in 1998. From 2004 to 2008, Danfoss's sales to these exporting producers grew by about 290%. In the same period, total sales for Danfoss China grew by 364%. In addition, after 2005, Danfoss's growth in sales was higher than the industry's overall growth (see Exhibit 6).

Approaching the mid-segment market
Two particular insights led Clausen to raise the targeted growth rates for the Chinese activities. One was that while some manufacturers would be very pleased with a 40% growth rate in China per year, market shares would be lost if market growth was actually 80%. The other came as he was travelling with his wife along the old Silk Road leading from Kazakhstan to Ürümqi in western China. Crossing the border from the rather primitive conditions in Kazakhstan into northwestern China, he realized that even far from coastal China, which was normally associated with the country's tremendous growth rates, the infrastruc-

ture was highly modern and well organized. In Ürümqi, he was, in particular, struck by seeing "a refrigerator with inverters that control the speed of the motor and thus save energy – a luxury category that one wouldn't find even in a large Danish town".[184]

It was, therefore, decided that the mid-segment market should be examined. The results showed that Danfoss appeared to be merely "skimming the surface". In simply transferring its European product range to China, Danfoss had apparently ignored a huge mid-segment market, which represented 70% of the total market and which grew twice as fast as the high-end market. In this huge market, Chinese producers and competitors were preparing themselves for growth and global expansion. They were able to build competences, brands and economies of scale in production. Leaving the Chinese producers alone to maneuver in this large mid-segment market posed a serious threat to Danfoss, not only in China, but also globally. As Mogens Terp Paulsen, CEO of Danfoss China, noted, "it is not wise to ignore the mid-end market. It's the biggest in China and it is the market segment where our future competitors will evolve. The risk is that our Chinese competitors – over time – amputate us, first in China and later on in other markets, when they also begin to produce high-end products".[185]

Danfoss China, therefore, deliberately incorporated the mid-segment market into its Chinese strategy. Indeed, it was expected that one-third of Danfoss's growth in China would be achieved through products developed specifically for the fast-growing Chinese mid-segment market. As part of the mid-segment strategy, Danfoss adopted a two-pronged investment strategy, with total Chinese investment amounting to about DKK 330 million in 2008 – an increase of 122% from 2007. On the one hand, the strategy entailed undertaking product development in China for Chinese customers. On the other hand, the strategy was to invest in Chinese companies that fit with Danfoss's product lines and were already operating in the mid-segment market. The desired outcome of this entry strategy would be the establishment of business relations with customers that were different from the company's traditional customers. For instance, within refrigeration, Danfoss was a global supplier to major international supermarkets such as Wal-Mart, Carrefour and Tesco. By entering the Chinese mid-segment market, it would be able to access domestic Chinese chains and supermarkets that were not interested in the high-end, expensive products. These mid-segment Chinese chains were expected to become a major source of increased sales in China.

In pursuing its strategy of investing in Chinese companies, Danfoss acquired a number of firms that were already established and operating in the mid-segment, and whose integration into Danfoss could facilitate entry into the mid-market. One such investment was the acquisition of Chinese Holip, which was a producer of frequency converter – a product belonging to the Motion Control division range (see Exhibit 3). Another was a joint venture with Qinbau, which produced heat exchangers. A final example was the joint venture with Tianjin Sanhua Refrigeration Equipment Co., Ltd., which had the largest sales and distribution network in China in commercial cooling equipment. This joint venture could open up the large mid-segment market of Chinese retail food stores.

In contrast to the more expensive high-end market, a salient feature of the mid-end segment was that it merely required "good enough" products. This meant, among other things, that product durability beyond what was expected was not viewed as an important feature. The new mid-segment products would, therefore, typically have fewer features, be less accurate and have shorter lifespans. Offering such products was seen as an inevitable response to customer demands.

In order to realize the opportunities inherent in adapting existing lines of high-end Danfoss products to the Chinese mid-segment, a special product development workforce was organized in Danfoss China. The product development team – where the number of staff was expected to triple within 18 months – would review the Danfoss product catalogue to find products that could be adapted to the Chinese mid-end market through changes in specifications. By early 2009, Danfoss was undertaking around a dozen product development projects – most of them in the refrigeration – all of which were based on investigations of the market and customer needs. One example of such a product was a refrigeration electronics product for supermarkets, which was introduced in 2009. The modified product controlled only four compressors and ventilators, as opposed to the ten controls offered by the conventional Danfoss products. Furthermore, it only controlled refrigeration, and not lighting or other aspects. Another product development project targeting the Chinese mid-end market was a water-heating system for Chinese hairdressers, which promised up to 70% savings on annual energy bills. This project was actually a result of an internal competition among employees to develop and present new innovative business ideas for Danfoss (also called the "Man on the Moon" project).[186]

However lucrative this mid-segment seemed, there was a risk that the downscaled versions of traditionally high-end, more expensive products might harm Danfoss's reputation in terms of delivering high-quality products. Yet, the company stressed that there was a significant difference between low quality low-end market and the Chinese mid-segment. Therefore, the company did not view the Chinese strategy as a threat to its high-end products. Rather, it was developing and introducing a line of products that could be offered at lower prices because they entailed fewer features. Danfoss could thereby reach a group of customers with different, less-stringent demands than the high-end customers to whom Danfoss had traditionally been catering. However, the company had no plans to begin selling mid-end products in markets outside China.[187]

Lobbying and IPR

Maintaining strong relations with Chinese authorities had always been a crucial task for Danfoss's management. This had included intense, continuous lobbying efforts aimed at Chinese officials. Among others things, Danfoss welcomed the Chinese ambassador to Denmark to Danfoss in 1997 despite the ongoing heated public debate in Denmark about Chinese human rights issues. Danfoss also actively lobbied Chinese policy makers in an attempt to influence the pricing system for energy consumption, which was based on the size of households' living areas rather than actual energy consumption.

Another aspect of Danfoss's relations with Chinese authorities was related to IPR efforts. Notoriously known for copying brand names, Chinese counterfeiters had been met with active countermeasures undertaken by Danfoss in close collaboration with Chinese authorities. Danfoss offered training to Chinese customs officers and facilitated raids on Chinese vendors offering products associated with the Danfoss range. One catch at a Chinese port alone resulted in the confiscation of 6,900 filter dryers used in refrigeration and air conditioning.

* * *

As Danfoss attempted to successfully settle in the large Chinese mid-end market, the question remained as to whether it would end up being forced to stick to the "high road" of its high-quality, premium brand or whether it could be able to solidly establish itself in this vast, growing mid-segment. The mid-end market not only seemed to offer considerable sales potential, but it was also alluring for local entrepreneurial firms, which were eager to build their own range of "good-enough" products that could undermine Danfoss if it failed to meet the challenge. As the world held its breath in the face of the global financial recession, Danfoss was considering whether to further leverage its debt exposure in order to capitalize on advantageous prices for possible acquisition targets in China. CFO Frederick Lotz explained that "historically, we have always taken market shares during bad periods".[188] However, Danfoss's Chinese competitors were also waiting for the right moment to buy.

Exhibits for Danfoss case

Exhibit 1 – Danfoss's key figures [189]

Financial highlights (EUR)					
	2003	2004	2005	2006	2007
PROFIT AND LOSS ACCOUNT					
Netsales	2,077	2,197	2,203	2,605	2,979
Operating profit added depreciations, amortisations and impairments (EBITDA)	268	235	228	325	346
EBIT excl. other income, etc.	103	122	123	189	219
Operating profit (EBIT)	149	144	127	215	217
Income from associates and joint ventures after tax	7	13	11	12	28
Financial items, net	-19	-32	-3	-39	-60
Profit before tax	138	125	135	188	185
Net profit	102	94	99	139	143
BALANCE SHEET					
Total non-current assets	801	873	1,027	1,359	1,482
Total assets	1,757	1,761	1,952	2,486	2,663
Equity	970	1,029	1,137	1,212	1,307
Net interest-bearing debt	51	22	111	384	501
Net assets	902	942	1,122	1,44	1,64
Capital expenditure	265	203	250	456	259
CASH FLOW STATEMENT					
Cash flow from operating activities	173	166	160	177	136
Cash flow from investing activities	-158	-128	-218	-405	-214
hereof acquisition of intangible and tangible fixed assets	-97	-173	-138	-122	-188
hereof acquisition of subsidiaries and activities	-51	48	-68	-260	-42
Free cash flow before M&A	74	-7	10	53	-57
Free cash flow	15	38	-58	-228	-77
Cash flow from financing activities	-56	-95	24	252	58
NUMBER OF EMPLOYEES					
Number of employees (headcount)	17,449	17,543	18,168	20,612	22,323
CONVERSION FACTOR BETWEEN DKK AND EUR					

Strategies in emerging markets

Profit and loss account and cash flow statement (average exchange rate 100 EUR)	743.07	743.98	745.19	745.91	745.06
Balance sheet (exchange rate at 31 December, 100 EUR)	744.46	743.81	746.05	745.60	745.66
KEY FIGURES					
EBIT margin excl. other income, etc.	5.0%	5.6%	5.6%	7.3%	7.4%
EBIT margin	7.2%	6.6%	5.8%	8.2%	7.3%
Adjusted EBIT margin	7.5%	6.9%	5.8%	8.4%	7.6%
EBITDA margin	12.9%	10.7%	10.4%	12.5%	11.6%
RONA	17.0%	15.6%	12.3%	16.8%	14.1%
Return on equity	10.8%	9.4%	9.2%	11.9%	11.4%
Equity ratio	55.2%	58.4%	58.2%	48.6%	49.0%
Leverage ratio	5.2%	2.2%	9.7%	31.8%	38.4%
Dividend ratio	12.5%	15.0%	18.0%	20.0%	25.0%

In the case where the Danish Association of Financial Analyst defines the above ratios, the ratios are computed according to these definitions.

Exhibit 2 – Danfoss's organization[190]

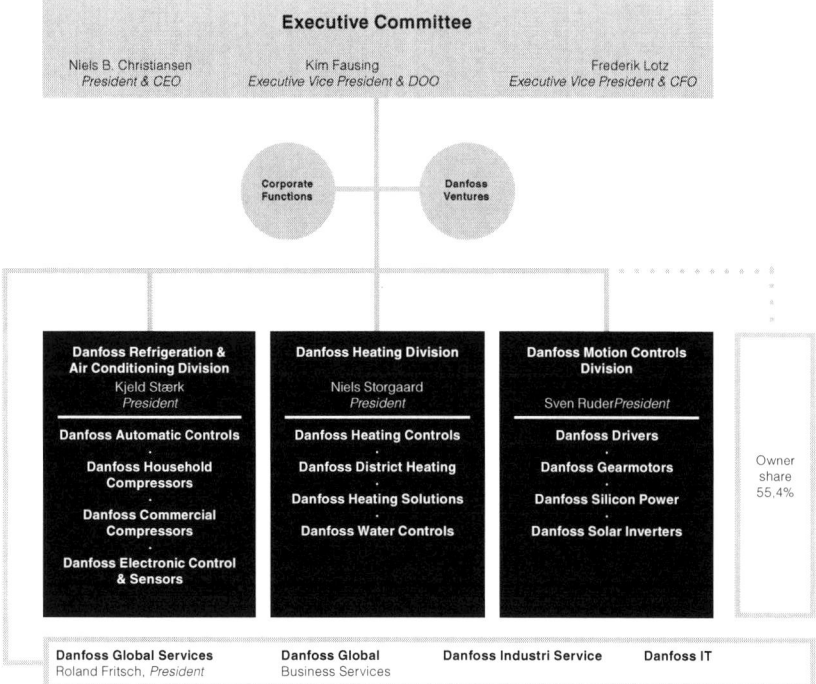

Strategies in emerging markets

Exhibit 3 – Product range[191]

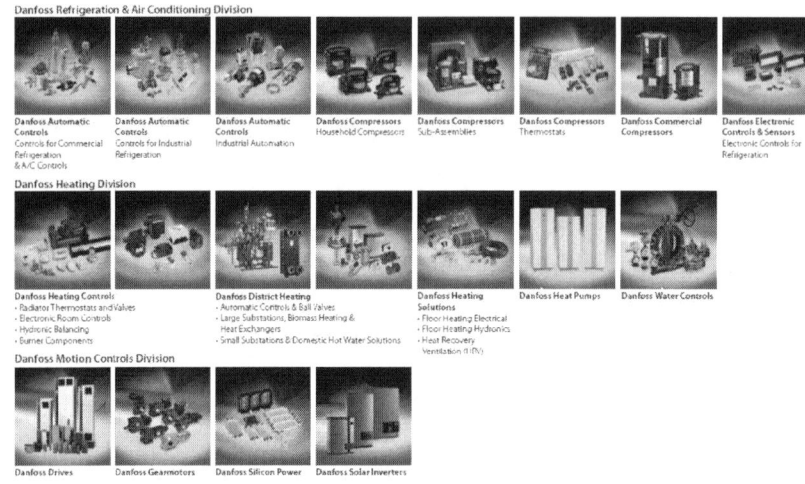

Exhibit 4 – Danfoss China organization[192]

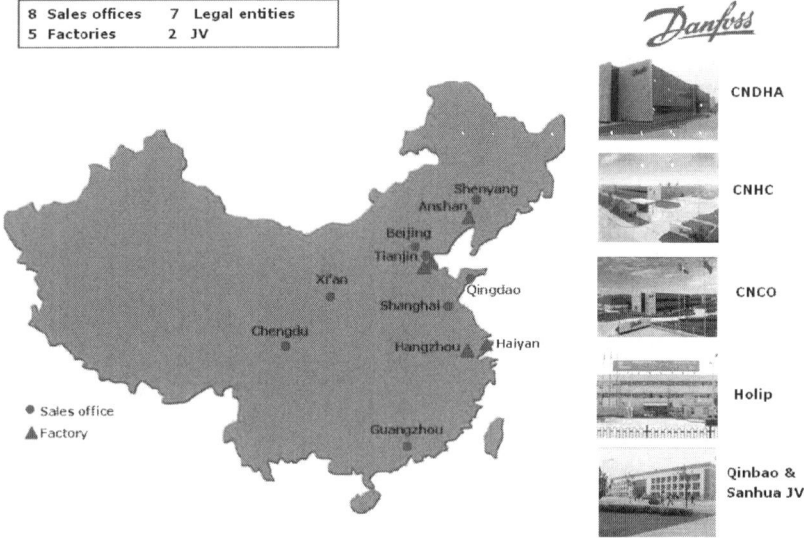

Exhibit 5 – Danfoss China key figures[193]

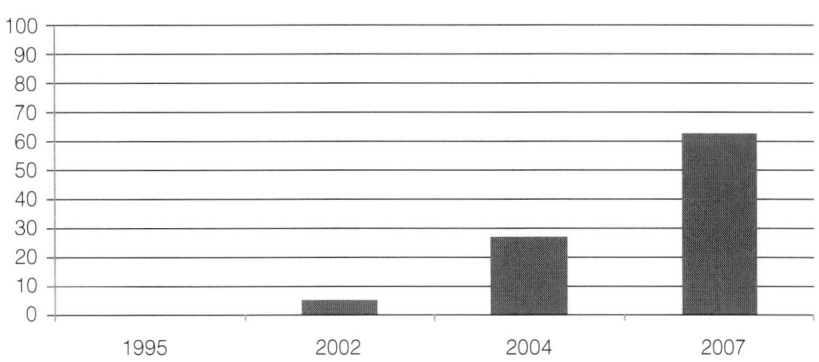

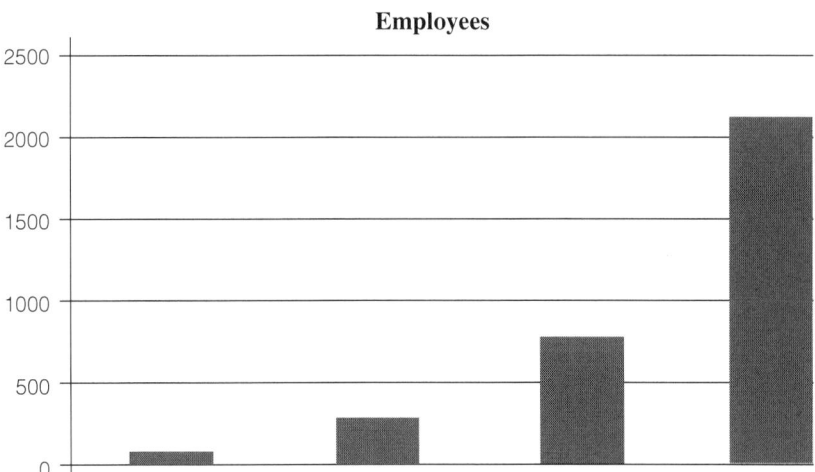

Strategies in emerging markets

Internal sales (mRMB)

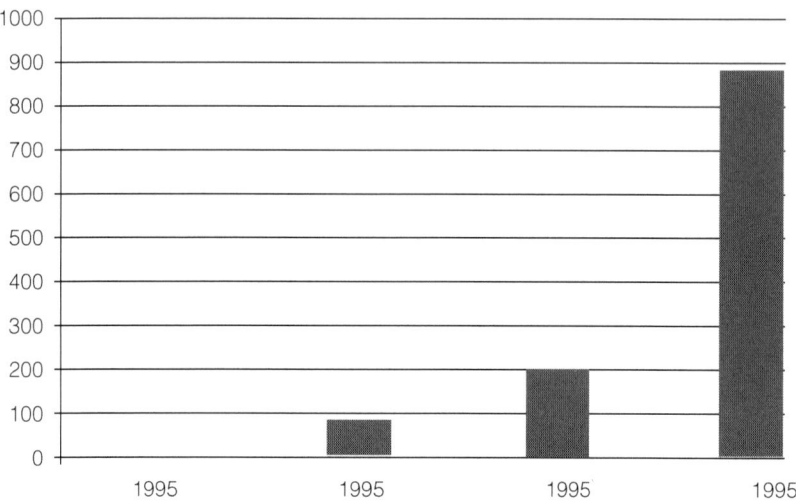

Note: Internal sales here refers to goods manufactured in China for Danfoss sales companies outside China. External sales are those direct to external customers which are invoiced from China.

External sales (mRMB)

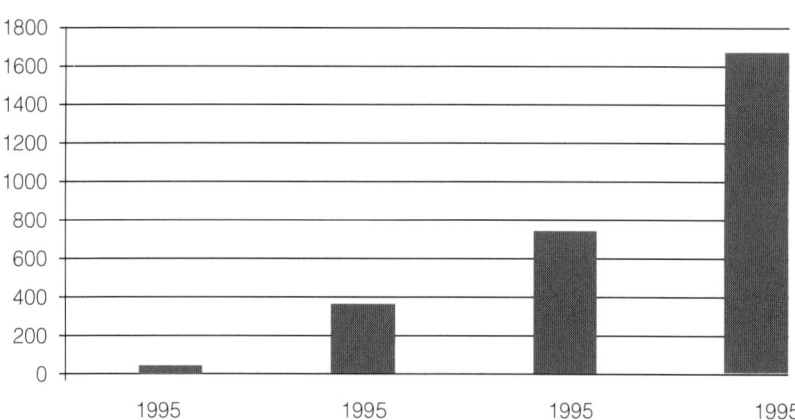

Note: Internal sales here refers to goods manufactured in China for Danfoss sales companies outside China. External sales are those direct to external customers which are invoiced from China.

Exhibit 6 – Relative increase in sales, 2004 to estimated 2008 (index: 2004)[194]

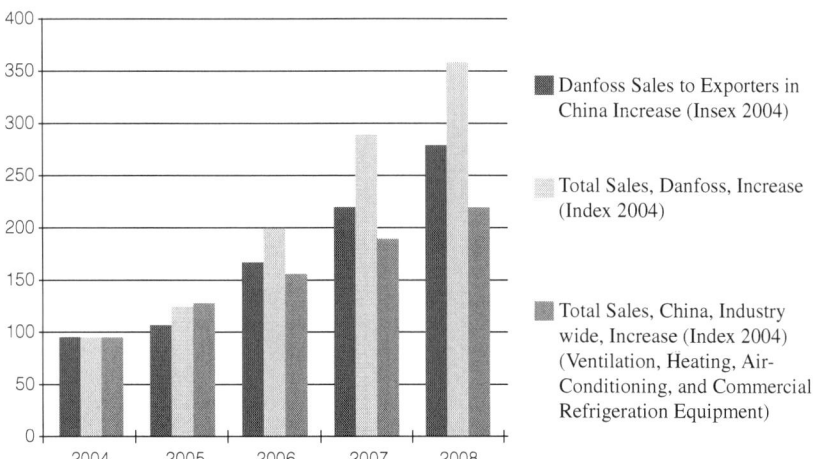

List of references

Anderson, E. & Gatignon, H. (1986). Modes of foreign entry: A transaction cost analysis and propositions. *Journal of International Business Studies*, 17(1): 1-26.

Arnold, D.J. & Quelch, J.A. (1998). New Strategies in Emerging Markets. *Sloan Management Review* 40(1): 7-20.

Aussilloux, V. (2000). *Foreign Direct Investment under Uncertainty: Option Value and Pre-emption Value*. Mimeo.

Batra, Rajeev (1997). Marketing Issues and Challenges in Transition Economies. *Journal of International Marketing,* 5(4): 95-114.

Birkinshaw, J., Hood, N. (1998). Multinational subsidiary evolution: capability and charter change in foreign-owned subsidiary companies. *Academy of Management Review* 23(4): 773– 795.

Brink, Jan, et al. (2005), *China Success: A Gateway to Global Success?*, Stockholm University School of Business, Autumn 2005.

Buckley, A. (1986). *Multinational finance*. Oxford, U.K.: Philip Allan.

Buckley, P.J. & Ghauri, P. (2004). Globalization, Economic Geography and the Strategy of MNEs. *Journal of International Business studies,* 35(2): 81-98.

Buckley, P.J. & Casson, M. (1976). *The future of the multinational enterprise.* London: Macmillan.

Cavusgil, S., Ghaury, P. & Agarwal, M. (2002). *Doing Business in Emerging Markets*. London: Sage.

Dawar, N. and A. Chattopadhay (2002) Rethinking Marketing Programs for Emerging Markets. *Long Range Planning* 35: 457-474.

Dicken, P. (2004) *Global Shift,* London: Sage.

Doh, P. J. (2005). Offshore outsourcing: Implications for International Business and Strategic Management Theory and Practice., *Journal of Management Studies*, 42(3): 695-704.

Dossani, R. & Kenney, M. (2007). The next wave of globalization: Relocating service provision to India. *World Development*, 35(5): 772-91.

Dunning, J. (1988). *Explaining international production*. London: Unwin-Hyman.

Douglas, S. & Craig. S. (1989). Evolution of Global Marketing Strategy: Scale, Scope and Synergy. *Columbia Journal of World Business*, 24(3): 47- 59.

Farrell, D. (2005). Offshoring: Value Creation through Economic Change. *Journal of Management Studies, 42(3): 675-683.

Grant, R.M., Almeida, P. and Song, J. (2000). Knowledge and the Multinational Enterprise. In C. Millar (Eds.), *International Business: Emerging Issues and Merging Markets.* London: Macmillan.

Greve, M., Hansen, M. & Schaumburg-Müller, H. (2007). *Container shipping and Economic Development: A Case study of A.P.Moller-Maersk.* Copenhagen: Copenhagen Business School Press.

Hamel, G., & Prahalad, C. K. (1985). Do you really have a global strategy? *Harvard Business Review*, 63(4): 139–148.

Hennart, J.F. (1991). The Transaction Cost Theory of the Multinational Enterprise. In C. Pitelis & C. Sudgen (Eds.), *The nature of the Transnational Firm.* London: Routledge.

Hobday, M. (1995). East Asian Latecomer Firms: Learning the Technology of Electronics. *World Development,* 23(7): 1171-1193.

Hoenen, A. & Hansen, M. (2009). *Oligopolistic competition and foreign direct investment: (Re-) Integrating the strategic management perspective in the theory of multinational corporations.* CBDS Working paper no 10, 2009.

Hofstede, G. (1983). The Cultural Relativity of Organizational Practices and Theories. *Journal of International Business Studies*, 14(2): 75-89.

Hoskisson, R., Hitt, M. Wan, W. & Yiu, D. (1999). Theory and research in strategic management: Swings of a pendulum *Journal of Management,* 25(3): 417–456.

Hoskisson, R., Eden, L., Lau, C. M. & Wright, M. (2000). Strategy in Emerging Economies. *Academy of Management Journal,* 43:249–67.

Jansson, H. (2007). *International Business Strategy in Emerging Country Markets. The Institutional Network Approach.* Aldershot: Edward Elgar.

Jensen, P. Ø. (2008). *Offshoring of advanced and high value technical services: Antecedents, process dynamics and firm level impacts.* Department of Intercultural Communication and Management Copenhagen Business School.

Johanson, J., & Vahlne, J.E. (1977/1998). The Internationalization Process of the Firm. In L. Engwall, *Four Decades of Uppsala Business Research.* Uppsala: University of Uppsala Press.

Kekic, L. (2009). The global economic crisis and FDI flows to emerging markets. *Columbia FDI Perspectives:Perspectives on topical foreign direct investment issues.* Written by the Vale Columbia Center on Sustainable International Investment, No. 15, October 8, 2009.

Khanna, T. & Palepu, K. (2006) Emerging Giants: Building World Class Companies in Emerging Economies. *Harvard Business Review*, 84(10): 60-69.

Khanna, T., & Palepu, K. (1997). Why Focused Strategies May Be Wrong for Emerging Markets. *Harvard Business Review,* 75(4): 3–10.

Kogut, B. (1985). Designing global strategies: Comparative and competitive

value-added chains. *Sloan Management Review, 27(Summer)*: 15–28.
Kogut, B. & Zander, U. (1993). Knowledge of the Firm and the Evolutionary Theory of the Multinational Corporation, *Journal of International Business Studies*, 24(4): 625-45.
Kolk A. & Tulder, R. (2005). Setting new global rules? TNCs and codes of conduct. *Transnational Corporations*, 14(3):1–27.
Kolk, A. & Tulder, R. (2006). Poverty Alleviation as Business Strategy? Evaluating Commitments of Frontrunner Multinational Corporations. *World Development,* 34(5): 789–801.
Kostova, T., Roth, K., & Dacin, M. T. (2008). Institutional theory in the study of multinational corporations: A critique and new directions. *Academy of Management Review*, 33(4): 994–1006.
Kotler, P. (1984). *Marketing Management, Analysis, Planning, and Control.* Englewood Cliffs, NJ: Prentice-Hall.
Lasserre, P (2007). *Global Strategic Management.* New York: Palgrave Macmillan.
Levitt, Theodore (1983). The Globalisation of Markets. *Harvard Business Review,* 61(3): 92-103.
London, T. & Hart, S.L. (2004). Reinventing Strategies for Emerging Markets: Beyond the Transnational Model. *Journal of International Business studies,* 35(5): 350–370.
Lung Y. (2000). Is the Rise of Emerging Countries as Automobile Producers an Irreversible Phenomenon? In J. Humphrey, Y. Lecler & M. Salerno (Eds), *Global Strategies and Local Realities: The Auto Industry in Emerging Markets* (16-41). London: Macmillan Press & New York: St Martin's Press.
Luo, Y. (2001). Toward a Cooperative View of MNC-Host Government Relations: Building Blocks and Performance Implications. *Journal of international business studies.* 32(3): 401-419.
Madhok, A. (1997). Cost, value and foreign market entry mode: The transaction and the firm. *Strategic Management Journal*, 18(1): 39–61.
Mathews, J. (2006) Dragon Multinationals: New Players in 21st century Globalization. *Asia Pacific Journal of Management* 23(1): 5-27.
McDougall, P. & Oviatt, B. (1994). Toward a Theory of International New Ventures. Journal of International Business Studies, 25(1): 45-64.
Metters R, & Verma, R. (2008). History of offshoring knowledge Services. *Journal of Operations Management,* 26(6): 141-147.
Meyer, K.E. & Tran, Y.T.T. (2006). Market penetration and acquisition strategies for emerging economies, *Long Range Planning*, 39(2): 177-197.
Mintzberg, H. (1994). The fall and rise of strategic planning. *Harvard Business Review,* 72(1):107-114.
Morisset, J. & Neso (2002). Administrative barriers to foreign investment in

developing countries. *Transnational Corporations*, 11(2): 99-121.

Mudambi, R. (1995). The MNE Investment Location Decision: Some Empirical Evidence. *Managerial and decision economics*,16(3):249-257.

Napier, N. K. & Vu, V.T. (1998). International Human Resource Management in Developing and Transitional Economy Countries: A Breed Apart? *Human Resource Management Review,* 8(1): 39-77.

Nielsen, C. (2005). The global chess game ... or is it go? Market-entry strategies for emerging markets., *Thunderbird International Business Review,* 47(4): 397-427.

Oetzel, J. & Doh, J. (2009). MNEs and development: a review and re-conceptualization. *Journal of World Business,* 44(2):108–120.

Patterson, S. & Brock, D. (2002). The Development of Subsidiary Management Research: Review and Theoretical Analysis. *International Business Review*, 11(2): 139-163.

Pedersen, T. (2009) *Vestas Wind systems A/S: Exploiting Global R&D Synergies.* SMG WP 5/2009. Frederiksberg: CBS

Peng, M., Wang, D. & Jiang, Y. (2008). An institution-based view of international business strategy: a focus on emerging economies. *Journal of International Business Studies,* 39: 920–936

Peng, M. (2002). Towards an Institution-Based View of Business Strategy. *Asia Pacific Journal of Management,* 19(4): 251–267.

Peng, M. (2003). Institutional Transitions and Strategic Choices. *The Academy of Management Review,* 28(2): 275-296.

Porter, M.E. (1986). Competition in Global Industries: A Conceptual Framework. In: M- Porter (eds.), *Competition in Global Industries* (15-60). Cambridge, MA: Harvard Business School.

Prahalad, C.K. & Hammond, A. (2002). Serving the World's Poor, Profitably. *Harvard Business Review,* 80(9): 48-58.

Pyndt, Jacob, and T. Pedersen (2006), "ECCO A/S – Optimizing Global Value Chain Economics", in Pyndt and Pedersen (2006), *Managing global offshoring strategies: A case approach.* Copenhagen: CBS Press.

Rahman, Z., & Bhattacharyya, S. K. (2003). First mover advantages in emerging economies: a discussion. *Management Decision*, 41(2): 141–147.

Ramamurti, R. (2000). Risks and rewards in the globalization of telecommunications in emerging economies. *Journal of World Business*, 35(2): 149–170.

Ramamurti, R. and J. Singh (2009). *Emerging Multinationals in Emerging Markets.* Cambridge: Cambridge University Press.

Sako, M. (2005). *Outsourcing and Offshoring: Key Trends and Issues.* Background Paper prepared for the Emerging Markets Forum in November 2005: Said School of Business.

Schenk, H. (1999). *Large mergers a matter of strategy rather than economics.*

List of references

Text box prepared for the UNCTAD's World Investment Report 1999, http://www2.econ.uu.nl/users/schenk/WIR99.html

Scott-Kennel, J. & Enderwick, P. (2005). FDI and Inter-firm Linkages: Exploring the Black Box of the IDP. *Transnational Corporations,* 14(1): 105-130.

Shapiro, A. (2002). Capital budgeting for the multinational corporation. Chapter 17 in *Foundations of Multinational Financial Management*: 477-508.

Shen, J. (2005). International training and management development: theory and reality. *The Journal of Management Development,* 24(7): 656-666.

Smarzynska, B. (1998). *Composition of FDI and Protection of Intellectual Property Rights in Transition Economies.* Yale University, mimeo.

Stabell, C. B. & Fjeldstad, Ø. D. (1998). Configuring value for competitive advantage: On chains, shops, and networks. *Strategic Management Journal,* 19(5): 413-37.

Tallman, S. (2006). Global strategic management. In Hitt et al, (Eds.), *The Blackwell Handbook of Strategic Management.* Blackwell.

Tolentino, P. E. (2008). Explaining the competitiveness of multinational companies from developing economies: a critical review of the academic literature. *International Journal of Technology and Globalisation,* 4(1): 23-38.

Trompenaars, F. & Hampden-Turner, C. (1998). *Riding the waves of culture: understanding cultural diversity in global business,* New York: McGraw-Hill Publication.

Wright, M., Filatotchev, I. , Hoskisson, R. & Peng, M. (2005). Strategy Research in Emerging Economies: Challenging the Conventional Wisdom. *Journal of Management Studies,* 42(1): 1-34.

Yip, G.S. (1995). *Total global strategy: Managing for worldwide competitive advantage.* Englewoods Cliffs, NJ: Prentice-Hall

Yip, G.S. (1989). Global strategy…in a world of nations? *Sloan Management Review,* 31: 29 – 41.

Endnotes

1. The term "global strategy" is used broadly here to denote strategies that are placed on an internationalization-continuum. At one end of the continuum, we find "total global strategy", where a deep functional division of labor is pursued on a truly global scale (Yip, 1989; 1995). At the other end of the continuum, we find international strategies, where the integration of foreign activities is shallow and where the geographical scope of activities is limited (Dicken, 2004).
2. Emerging markets are understood as economies that have sustained high growth rates (typically annual GDP growth in excess of 5%), that are in the process of developing market institutions and structures, and that have reached a certain level of industrialization (see e.g., Arnold and Quelch, 1998). The definition of emerging markets is not 100% clear cut but is normally used to denote developing countries that are neither "least developed" nor "newly industrialized". The emerging market category typically includes the BRIC countries, countries in Southeast Asia and Latin America, and South Africa. It is debatable whether the Gulf States should be viewed as emerging markets because of their relatively weak market and industrial structures.
3. Business.dk, "Milliarder venter Carlsberg i Asien", 18/08 2008
4. Carlsberg Annual Report 2007
5. Carlsberg Annual Report 2007
6. Børsen, "Utålmodig brygger klar til nye revolutioner", 18/05 2007
7. Politiken, "Hellere bedst til tørst end størst" 04/04 2004
8. Børsen, "Orkla ville sluge Carlsberg" 01/02 2008
9. Børsen, "Carlsberg investerer tålmodigt i Kina", 11/10 2005
10. Carlsberg Annual Report 2007
11. Reuters, "Carlsberg ser positivt på InBevs køb af Anheuser-Busch", 14/07 2008
12. Børsen, "Carlsberg har ambitiøse mål for russisk marked", 19/03 2003
13. www.carlsberggroup.com
14. Børsen, "Carlsbergs russiske guldæg satser i Asien og Amerika", 12/06 2007
15. Børsen, "Carlsbergs russiske guldæg satser i Asien og Amerika", 12/06 2007
16. Børsen, "Carlsberg på kinesisk opkøbstogt", 16/7 2004
17. Jyllands-Posten, "Carlsberg åbner bryggeri i Vestkina", 30/7 2005
18. Carlsberg Annual Report 2007
19. business.dk, "Milliarder venter på Carlsberg i Asien", 18/8 2008
20. Jyllands-Posten, "Carlsberg taber penge på udvidelser i Kina", 12/10 2005
21. Carlsberg Annual Report 2007
22. Data collected from the www.carlsberg.com
23. Carlsberg Annual Report 2007
24. Carlsberg Annual Report 2007
25. www.ecco.com
26. www.ecco.com

27 Markedsføring, "Ecco 2.0", 26.08 2008
28 Ritzaus Bureau, "Ecco går frem i Asien", 04.09 2008
29 Pyndt and Pedersen (2006), "ECCO A/S – Optimizing Global Value Chain Economics"
30 Fyns Amt Avis, "Fra koen til skoen", 17.09 2008
31 The ECCO Code of Conduct 2007
32 Jv.dk, "Ecco sætter nye standarder med læderfabrik", 06.09 2008
33 Leather365.com, "Opening of ECCO's China tannery", 28/07 2009
34 Børsen, "Ecco åbner fem fabrikker i Kina", 04.08 2009
35 Fyns Amt Avis, "Fra Koen til Skoen", 17.09 2008
36 Jyllands-Posten, "Interview: Ecco gik egne veje i Kina", 18.10 2005
37 Jyllands-Posten, "Ecco-chef: Forfejlet IFU-kritik", 18.10 2005
38 Jyllands-Posten, "Interview: Ecco gik egne veje i Kina", 18.10 2005
39 Ritzaus Bureau, "Ecco udvider med garveri i Kina", 05.09 2008
40 JydskeVestkysten, "JV i Xiamen: Ecco-ansatte får årslønn på 12.700 kr", 11.09 2008
41 JydskeVestkysten, "Ecco afviser ny production i billig-land", 06.09 2008
42 JydskeVestkysten, "Ecco afviser ny production i billig-land", 06.09 2008
43 Berlingske Tiderne, "Ecco stopper øjeblikkeligt udvidelse i Kina", 05.10 2006
44 Ritzaus Bureau, "Ecco går frem i Kina", 04.09 2008
45 ECCO Annual Report 2008
46 ECCO Annual Report 2008
47 ECCO Annual Report 2008
48 Pyndt and Pedersen (2006), "ECCO A/S – Optimizing Global Value Chain Economics"
49 "A Blueprint for the African Leather Industry — a development, investment and trade guide for the leather industry in Africa", UNIDO 2004, p. 17
50 ECCO internal illustration
51 ECCO Annual Report 2008
52 The ECCO Code of Conduct 2007
53 ECCO Annual Report 2008
54 www.flsmidth.com: sales, engineering and project execution services
55 Investor presentation, LD Markets, Billund, 12.01.2009, from FLSmidth homepage
56 FLSmidth Annual Report 2007, p. 4
57 Investor presentation, Gemini Large Cap Seminar, 22.09 2008, p. 3, from FLSmidth homepage
58 FLSmidth Annual Report 2007, p. 15
59 RB-Børsen 16.03 2009
60 FLSmidth Annual Report 2007, p. 5
61 Jyllands-Posten, 07.10 1999
62 Berlingske Nyhedsmagasin, 02.03 2007
63 Ministry of Foreign Affairs of Denmark: The Trade Council, India "Fremtidens FLS starter i Indien". 12.06 2007
64 Ministry of Foreign Affairs of Denmark: The Trade Council, India "Fremtidens FLS starter i Indien". 12.06 2007
65 Berlingske Nyhedsmagasin, 02.03 2007
66 Horsens Folkeblad, 19.10 2007
67 MM Management 08

Endnotes

68 Horsens Folkeblad, 19.10 2007
69 Epn.dk, 06.05 2007
70 Berlingske Nyhedsmagasin, 02.03 2007
71 Epn.dk, 06.05 2007
72 Berlingske Nyhedsmagasin, 02.03 2007
73 Berlingske Nyhedsmagasin, 02.03 2007
74 Børsen 18.04.2005; Berlingske Tidende 27.04 2005
75 MM Management 08
76 FLSmidth Annual Report 2008
77 www.flsmidth.com
78 www.flsmidth.com
79 FLSmidth Annual Report 2008
80 Flsmidth Annual Report 2007
81 FLSmidth Annual Report 2007
82 www.flsmidth.com
83 Berlingske Tidende, "Kinesiske forbrugere er med fremme", 2007
84 Berlingske Tidende, "Kinesiske forbrugere er med fremme", 2007
85 www.bestseller.com
86 www.bestseller.com
87 Børsen Magasiner, "En simple vej til succes", 14.04 2004
88 Berlingske Tidende, "Interview: Bestseller går globalt", 13/02 2005; Anders Holch Povlsen Interview, pp. 14-15; Børsen (2002) "Mellemøsten nyt vækstområde"
89 Berlingske Tidende, "Interview: Bestseller går globalt", 13/02 2005
90 Berlingske Tiderne, "Interview: Bestseller går globalt", 13.02 2005
91 Detailbladet, "Bestseller tjener mere på at sælge billigere", 21/1 2002
92 Børsen,"Bestseller tæt på milliard-resultat", 2002
93 Brink, Jan, et al., *China Success: A Gateway to Global Success?,* Stockholm University School of Business, Autumn 2005
94 Børsen,"Bestseller åbner egne butikker i Kina", 1997
95 Deloitte, "China's Consumer Market – Opportunities and Risks", 2005, p. 2
96 www.oanda.com – converted from DKK to EUR per 14.7.2008
97 Børsen, "Dansk modetøj bestseller i Kina", 1998
98 Deloitte, "China's Consumer Market – Opportunities and Risks", 2005, p. 5
99 Brink, Jan, et al., *China Success: A Gateway to Global Success*
100 Brink, Jan, et al., *China Success: A Gateway to Global Success*
101 Jyllands Posten, "Kinesere går i dansk modetøj", 11.08.2004
102 Brink, Jan, et al., *China Success: A Gateway to Global Success*
103 Brink, Jan, et al., *China Success: A Gateway to Global Success*
104 Jyllands Posten, "Kinesere går i dansk modetøj", 11.08 2004
105 Brink, Jan, et al., *China Success: A Gateway to Global Success*
106 www.business.dk, "Kampen om de modebevidste kineserne", 15.04 2007
107 Berlingske Tiderne, "IC Companys åbner i Kina", 17.03 2005
108 www.business.dk, "Kampen om de modebevidste kineserne", 15.04 2007
109 Brink, Jan, et al., *China Success: A Gateway to Global Success*
110 HK Edition (2005) "Sewing seam of gold in tough market", p. 2
111 www.giordano.com
112 Brink, Jan, et al., *China Success: A Gateway to Global Success*
113 Brink, Jan, et al., *China Success: A Gateway to Global Success*

Strategies in emerging markets

114 Brink, Jan, et al., *China Success: A Gateway to Global Success*
115 Greens online
116 www.bestseller.com
117 www.bestseller.com
118 MENTEL report
119 MENTEL report
120 Bestseller Annual Report 2007/06
121 www.bestseller.com
122 www.bestseller.com
123 Greens online
124 www.iccompanys.com
125 www.brandtex.com
126 www.gapinc.com, www.hm.com, www.inditex.com
127 www.gapinc.com
128 Financial figures converted to USD from SEK on 09.07 2008 (www.oanda.com)
129 Financial figures are collected from Inditex, Zara's mother company. Financial figures converted to USD from EUR on 09.07 2008 (www.oanda.com)
130 www.bestseller.com
131 IFU Homepage
132 Figures for 2007 are based on estimates from Jyllands-Posten (2007) "Bestseller spurter frem", as well as own estimates. Figures from 2006 are based on Børsen (2006) "Bestseller strammer konceptet til", as well as own estimates
133 Brink, Jan, et al., *China Success: A Gateway to Global Success*
134 Berlingske Tidende, "A.P. Møller satser stort i Vietnam", 03.08 2006
135 Berlingske Tidende, "A.P. Møller satser stort i Vietnam", 03.08 2006
136 Greve et al. (2007), "Container shipping and economic development", p. 25
137 Greve et al. (2007), "Container shipping and economic development", p. 30
138 Greve et al. (2007), "Container shipping and economic development", p. 27
139 Greve et al. (2007), "Container shipping and economic development", p. 27
140 Greve et al. (2007), "Container shipping and economic development", p. 17
141 Greve et al. (2007), "Container shipping and economic development", p. 37
142 Greve et al. (2007), "Container shipping and economic development", p. 31
143 Greve et al. (2007), "Container shipping and economic development", p. 42
144 Berlingske Tidende, "A.P. Møller satser stort i Vietnam", 03.08 2006
145 Greve et al. (2007), "Container shipping and economic development", p. 26
146 Greve et al. (2007), "Container shipping and economic development", p. 32
147 Greve et al. (2007), "Container shipping and economic development", p. 6
148 A.P. Møller – Mærsk Annual Report 2008
149 A.P. Møller – Mærsk Annual Report 2008
150 Greve et al. (2007), "Container shipping and economic development", p. 7
151 Greve et al. (2007), "Container shipping and economic development", p. 16
152 Greve et al. (2007), "Container shipping and economic development", p. 10
153 Maersk Line includes Safmarine and P&O NL; APL includes NOL; CMA-CGM includes ANL-CL and Ybarra; Evergreen includes Hatsu Marine and Lloyd Triesstino; Hanjin includes Senator; NYK includes TSK
154 Press release No 15/2006 from Vestas Asia Pacific A/S
155 Jyllands-Posten 30.10 1999
156 Politiken 08.12 1999
157 direct-dk 15.11 2005

Endnotes

158 Vestas Wind, No. 6, 2006
159 direkt-dk 05.09 2006
160 Vestas Wind, No. 6, 2006
161 Pedersen, T. (2009) 'Vestas Wind systems A/S: Exploiting Global R&D Synergies' *SMG WP 5/2009*. Frederiksberg: CBS
162 RB-Børsen 2006 10 16; Press release no. 11/2006 from Vestas Asia Pacific A/S
163 direkt-dk 09.01 2006
164 Stiften.dk 01.10 2005
165 direct-dk 15.11 2005
166 Vestas India Presentation, Michael Høghdal, Chennai
167 Vestas Info Kit, www.vestas.com
168 Vestas Annual Report 2008
169 Vestas Wind, November 2006
170 BTM Consult ApS, March 2008 (http://www.btm.dk)
171 Danfoss Annual Report 2007 p. 1
172 Danfoss Annual Report 2009 p. 46
173 Danfoss Annual Report 2007, p. 111
174 Jørgen M. Clausen Presentation, April 2007
175 Ingeniøren 03.10 2008
176 Business.dk 20.09 2008
177 Berlingske Tidende 27.03 2005
178 Der Nordschleswiger 24.09 2008
179 Jydske Vestkysten 24.09 2008
180 Global Danfoss 1/09, company publication: p. 5
181 Lotz, Nyhedsbrev for bestyrelser, 21.11 2008
182 McKinsey Quarterly, pp. 1-2
183 Jyllands-Posten 17.02 1998
184 McKinsey Quarterly
185 Global Danfoss. 01/09, p. 11
186 http://uk.danfossuniverse.com/page1506.aspx (last accessed 05.20 2010)
187 Global Danfoss. 01/09, p. 11
188 Nyhedsbrev for bestyrelser, 21.11 2008
189 Danfoss Annual Report 2007
190 Danfoss Annual Report 2007
191 Danfoss InfoKit, 2008
192 Stakeholder presentation, Mogens Terp Paulsen, 2008
193 Stakeholder presentation, Mogens Terp Paulsen, 2008
194 Stakeholder presentation, Mogens Terp Paulsen, 2008; EMIS Monthly Indicators, May 2008